Creation vs. Evolution

SECOND REVISED EDITION

Thomas F. Heinze

Baker Book House
Grand Rapids, Michigan

Foreword

In any field of knowledge a good handbook serves to distill essential facts and to dispel outworn theories and old wives' tales. On no topic is such a handbook so needed as in the matter of creation versus evolution.

It is a distinct pleasure then to welcome a new edition of Thomas Heinze's handbook on this subject. With solid facts gathered from many quarters, the theory of evolution is weighed in the balance and found wanting both in science and in logic.

At the same time, the facts marshalled here surely confirm as never before the trustworthiness of Scripture, the handiwork of the Creator, and the folly of the mind which persists in saying, "There is no God!"

Robert L. Whitelaw
Professor of Mechanical and
*   Nuclear Engineering*
Virginia Polytechnic Institute
*   and State University*

I have read with pleasure and profit your book, **Creation Versus Evolution Handbook.** Though relatively brief, your book covers comprehensively this important question of creation versus evolution. It is scientifically accurate and should be very helpful to all those who are open minded on this vital subject.

Duane T. Gish
Associate Director
Institute for Creation Research
San Diego, California

ISBN: 0-8010-4002-7

Copyright © 1973, by Baker Book House Company

First printing, July 1973
Second printing, April 1974
Third printing, November 1976

Printed in the United States of America

Introduction

It seemed as if a different boy stood before me. His attitude had changed from the arrogance and condescension of superior knowledge to a thoughtful silence, interrupted every few moments by another question. He had just realized for the first time in his life, that the fossil record of the horse, so often considered the clearest single evidence of evolution was the wrong kind of evidence! Though the evidence for a gradual change from four toes on the front legs and three on the back to just one toe on each, had been well presented to him, as to most students, as a proof of evolution, it really proved the wrong thing! It went from the complex to the simple! From more toes to less! Imagining a great extension of this kind of change, a horse could degenerate down to a single cell, but a single cell could never work its way up to becoming a horse or a person. In spite of this basic weakness, the horse is usually presented as one of the best evidences of evolution. It is in fact one of the best, not because it is good, but by comparison with the others.

Young people throughout the world are turning in ever increasing numbers to united riot and protest, or to individual withdrawal from a senseless, pointless world, which they believe got here by accident and is going no place. Their answer so far seems to consist more in the destruction of themselves and society as they know it than in anything else. They have not believed in evolution because of the strength of the evidence, but because, as was the case with the student mentioned above, they have heard virtually nothing on the other side and naturally assume that this means that there is no evidence to support the creation of the world by God. In reality though, there is good evidence to support God's creation, and instead of the student cited above in the conversation about the horse, many other people could have been mentioned in connection with any of the major areas of evidence. I think of a fuzzy faced college student who made appointments to talk with me in the library of his university in between his hours of work as a research assistant. His hair was long, and he was on dope, but his mind was not closed. He wanted to know.

The Bible says, "Ye shall know the truth, and the truth shall make you free." It is with the desire to get out the scientifically accurate truth in a compact well-rounded form that busy people can read, that this study was undertaken.

I would like to extend my sincere appreciation to the many who have helped make this book a possibility: the professors in the various scientific fields treated, who have given guidance and checked the scientific accuracy; the people who have helped in the research, typing, and proof reading. Without their help, this little handbook would have been impossible.

Thomas F. Heinze

c/o

Centro Biblico
Via Carriera Grande, 37
Naples, Italy

or

2405 First St.
Tillamook, Oregon
U.S.A.

Contents

1

Introduction to the Problem

A friend of mine who is a young medical doctor studying toward a Ph.D. recently had to repeat a course in biochemistry which he had taken just eight years before. It was not that he needed a refresher, or that he had not learned the subject well the first time. The reason was simply that biochemistry had changed so much in eight short years that the course he had taken no longer represented current thinking on the subject. "Practically everything that for years we believed to be true has been proven false or incorrect by subsequent discovery," said Prof. Edward Teller in a lecture at the University of California, in which he described the progress of science since World War II. "In fact there is only one statement that I would now dare to make positively: There is absolutely nothing faster than the speed of light—maybe."[1]

If the truth is absolute and always the same, then if it agreed completely with yesterday's science, it would not agree with today's, and if it agreed with today's it would not agree with tomorrow's. The fact that science is progressing in its findings and consequently changing its interpretations does not in any way reduce the value of science. We must recognize however that a given point of view is not necessarily scientifically incorrect just because it does not agree with a theory that many, or even all scientists hold at a given moment. On the contrary, any given standard

---

1. *Reader's Digest*, September 1970, p. 20.

that was in accord with every aspect of yesterday's science would be wrong by today's science, and one that was in agreement in every point with today's science would be shown wrong tomorrow. The idea of a time of creation is admittedly out of favor with much of scientific thinking today, but we will see after examining the evidence that there are good scientific reasons for it to come back in tomorrow.

In the hundred years since the theory of evolution first became popular, a veritable flood of scientific information has washed over its foundations, taking with it one pillar of its supporting structure after another, spontaneous generation and the heredity of acquired traits, to mention just two of the scientific "truths" of its day. While construction on the super-structure has never let up, and the fortress of evolution appears more impregnable than ever, it is time to take a good look at the foundations, and that is the purpose of this book.

The problem of whether the life around us has come about by God's creation or by evolution is too often seen as a question of science against religion. Most religious people, especially those who believe the Bible, fall into the creationist camp. A conclusion is then too often drawn that the other camp, that of evolution, is the scientific one. Since no one wants to seem unscientific, being taught that evolution is the scientific answer tends to sweep almost everyone blindly into the evolution camp. The scientific evidence that supports creation by God is almost never presented in modern education! It is the purpose of this book to help you get started in a critical examination of both the scientific facts that are presented as proofs of evolution and those which disprove it. The fact that the Bible teaches that God created the world, far from branding creation as an outmoded theory, is really a point in its favor since, though the Bible has been attacked more relentlessly through the centuries than any other book, it still stands today as the world's most powerful and influential force for good. Its position, instead of being weakened by the conflict and controversy of the past, has been strengthened. Where attack was made, point after point, the Bible has been proven true and the opposing theory false.

The Importance of Viewpoint

Some evidence when examined with the presupposition that God does not exist, or that He does not have effective contact with His creation, could logically support evolution. The same evidence examined from the viewpoint that He does exist often yields completely different conclusions.

When we are faced with evidence which can be explained in two different ways, it seems most unscientific to withhold consideration of one of these ways, just because it does not fit one's ideas of how something should have happened. This narrow approach, however, is exactly what is expected of every student in most of our school systems today where evolution is presented as a fact that all but the stupid and unscientific accept unquestionably. Some books even go so far as to state that it would be unscientific even to consider the other possibility.

But to be honest and to use the scientific method, we must also permit the student to examine the evidence from the "other" viewpoint, and such examination is the purpose of this book.

Before going ahead, we must distinguish between the facts, or evidence, that science has to work with and the interpretations of these facts.

The facts themselves are not in conflict with the Bible. The same facts or evidence used to support evolution may also be interpreted in such a way as to be in agreement with the Bible's description of creation. There are usually various possible interpretations of the same facts, and especially in this field,

11

where the evidence many times consists only of minute pieces of bone. The fact that different evolutionary scientists often differ among themselves, sometimes presenting many possible interpretations of the same evidence, shows clearly that the significance of the evidence is often not clear even to them.

There are also many instances of evolutionists having radically changed interpretations which were previously quite widely accepted. A good example is the Neanderthal man, who for years was presented as a stooped and stupid evolutionary link between upright walking man and the ape (or some common ancestor). Though for many years there have been many Neanderthal fossils available for study, only recently have evolutionists begun to replace his statues and pictures, and to admit that Neanderthal man stood erect, had a larger brain than we do, and was not a link in the evolutionary chain leading to man. When a man is convinced of the truth of an idea and is looking for evidence to prove it correct, his judgment tends to become biased, and he tends to interpret everything in a way which will prove his point.

The Philosophical Base of Evolution

How and why did the much-defended idea of evolution begin? At the time of Michelangelo and Leonardo daVinci a philosophic movement called *humanism* arose. Though some roots of evolutionistic thought can be traced farther back than this to Greek philosophy, it was humanism which popularized the philosophic basis of evolution.

Humanism came in the 1500s as a reaction against medieval theology and philosophy, which studied in great detail that which theologians said about that which other theologians had said about that which earlier theologians had said. Humanism instead went directly to the facts and to the oldest and most authoritative documents, whether of the Greek philosophers, or of the Bible, or of some other sources. Its emphasis was on man and man's importance and abilities. Humanism presented him as becoming better and better. One illuminating example of its expression is a group of statues by Michelangelo which shows men and women who seem to be forming themselves, and at the same time with their own tremendous force, tearing themselves loose from the rock from which they are carved. These striking statues illustrate as well as anything the tendency of humanism to minimize man's need of God, inferring that we have become that which we are by our own strength. A look at one of these statues gives a most forceful preview of the theory of evolution and shows that the philosophical groundwork had already been laid.

Rationalism followed humanism and added a disbelief in God and the miraculous, with its "I won't believe it if I can't see it!" attitude, applied especially to God and the supernatural.

Thus the groundwork was laid for Darwin to set forth a way in which living things could be explained apart from God's creating them. His idea was accepted because enough people were ready. The philosophy of the day had prepared their minds to accept his explanation.

Introduction to the Problems of Evolution

Kerkut[2] lists seven assumptions which form the "General Theory of Evolution," none of which can be experimentally verified:

1. Nonliving things gave rise to living material, i.e., spontaneous generation occurred.

2. Spontaneous generation occurred only once. (Additional assumptions follow from this one.)

3. Viruses, bacteria, plants, and animals are all interrelated.

---

2. G.A. Kerkut, *Implications of Evolution*, 1960, p. 6.

4. Protozoa gave rise to Metazoa.

5. The various invertebrate phyla are interrelated.

6. Invertebrates gave rise to the vertebrates.

7. Within the vertebrates the fish gave rise to the amphibia, the amphibia to the reptiles, and the reptiles to the birds and mammals. (Sometimes this last assumption is expressed in others words, e.g., modern amphibia and reptiles had a common ancestral stock.)

Kerkut, though an evolutionist himself, criticizes the general theory of evolution because of the lack of evidence to support its assumptions. He suggests the possibility of life having started several times, each giving rise to separate lines of plants and animals.

In addition to the problem of connections between the various kinds of plants and animals, evolution has no acceptable answer even today as to where the first life, or the universe itself for that matter, came from. The fact that it does not is shown by the large number of theories which are offered, each with its own proofs that its predecessors were wrong. This problem of beginnings, which could not be answered, has been overcome psychologically, however. It was postulated that the process took an incomprehensibly great number of years. The natural reaction when confronted with millions or billions of years is to assume that in that length of time anything could happen. Thus the basic problems could be left unanswered, hidden behind such a great mountain of years that no one would notice them. Men were freed to believe that which the philosophical notions of the day made them want to believe.

Since evolution does not provide the basic answers, while the Bible does, why then do so many scientists accept evolution? It is not because the Bible is in opposition to the facts of science. Though it is not in agreement with certain interpretations of the facts, it goes well with the facts themselves. Instead, it is because most scientists today reflect what they have been taught. Almost every textbook presents evolution as the sole intellectual possibility. In addition, there are probably a minority of scientists who actually understand that if they accept the Bible's account of creation then it follows that man is not pressing onward and upward to perfection, but has fallen into sin and needs to accept the salvation that God has provided for him in Jesus Christ. Pride and rebellion against this plan of God no doubt accounts for the readiness of some to turn to the evolutionary interpretation of the evidence.

Evolution is an attempt to explain from an atheistic viewpoint the existence of living things. Though only the evidence which tends to show evolution to be right is usually presented in our textbooks, there is no good reason why anyone should have to accept the theory without a chance to examine its defects. *Being presented as a fact does not make evolution a fact.* Instead, as we will see, it is so full of unanswered problems that those who accept it must accept it by faith. Even finding a method by which it could have taken place is so full of problems that it has driven some evolutionists to admit that evolution does not occur today, and yet they accept by faith that it must have occurred in the past. The majority, however, seeing the problems of this position would rather hold that it still occurs but so slowly as to be almost unobservable. Others have tried to explain away the difficulties by saying that evolution has produced the life which we see around us because God chose to use evolution to produce this life. This idea which attempts a syncretism between the two opposing theories of divine creation and evolution, is accepted neither by those who believe the Bible, nor by those who adopt the main line of evolutionary thinking.

We will examine the problems of the theory of evolution in more detail, but first let us look at its "proofs."

2

The Evidence Which Is Interpreted to Prove Evolution

The idea of evolution is that all of the plants and animals which we have today have gradually developed from a single simple cell billions of years ago. A movement from the simple to the complex is therefore necessary for this theory; for, although often used as a proof of evolution; it remains a fact that mere change that did not add complexity would have left us with only different one-celled animals (assuming that one-celled animals had begun the process), and could never have produced that which is attributed to evolution.

Evolution is believed by the evolutionists to have come about by natural selection, that is, the survival of the fittest working on chance variations. This will be discussed in more detail later. Suffice it to say here that every idea which is wrong must have a good deal that is right in it or it would never be accepted. This is as true of evolution as of anything else. The fact that there actually is a certain amount of natural selection does not, however, prove that all the plants and animals which exist today have come into existence by such means. That would be like saying "Mud is brown. Therefore, everything brown is muddy."

The facts fit better with God's explanation found in the Bible, that He created various general types of plants and animals and that these reproduce according to their general type. Natural selection working on these basic types could much more logically explain the variations which are actually found today than it could account for a movement from the simplest single cell to the most complex person living today.

Certain lines of proof are generally used to sustain the theory of evolution. We will now examine individually those which are most widely used.

Comparative Anatomy

You look like a monkey! Of course this is not completely true, but there are certainly some real similarities, though it is obvious that there are also many differences. Because of the resemblance, evolution says that either man evolved from the monkey or that both had a common ancestry.

Similarities can certainly indicate relationship, but not necessarily this relationship.

In front of me, as I write, are a number of books on the shelves. Among these are two which are almost identical. The covers are the same. The paper is of the same type. Only the thickness and the words inside are different. It is possible that one who knows little about books could conclude that the thicker one had evolved from the less thick one. The real reason for the similarity though is that they are of the same series by the same publisher. Evolution is only one of several possible reasons for similarity, and is not proved by similarity. Origin in the mind of the same designer is just as likely to be the real reason for similarity. Similarity of design is not logical evidence against a designer.

Another illustration is found in nature where one finds atoms to be similar to solar systems, only smaller. Both have a nucleus, with planets which revolve around it. No one, however, seriously suggests on the basis of comparative anatomy that the solar system evolved from the atom, because neither are living; yet the similarities are just as real as those which are used to prove evolutionary relationships. If the similarity

17

shows us anything, it is that the two originated in the mind of the same creator. In the same way, similarity in animal structure indicates creation by the same God.

Embryology

The so-called biogenetic law that "ontogeny recapitulates phylogeny" was one of the "proofs" used for evolution. The idea is that the embryo goes through the same stages in its development that human beings went though in their evolutionary process. In the past this argument has been used widely, but more recently *Encyclopedia Britannica* referred to it as a "gross oversimplification."[3] The evolutionist A. O. Woodford demolishes this one-time "proof" of evolution:

> But the implications as to lines of descent are not now taken seriously. The tiny genes in the first cell of a new individual contain the whole program for its later development. The genes are similar to the program fed into a computer, telling it what things to do and the order in which to do them. The program for the development of an individual organism may include a favorable variation from the previous norm, and the variation may become part of the distinctiveness of a new species. But only chance would produce a variation of the adult form and also produce at an immature stage the previous adult form.[4]

We must still examine the argument, however, since it is still often used, especially in the more elementary texts, which unfortunately have often been more interested in "selling" the theory than in the methods being used to sell it. They seem to take

---

3. Vol. 8, 1967, p. 318.
4. *Historical Geology*, 1965, p. 32.

18

much longer to drop a disproved "proof" of evolution than to add a new one.

Admittedly there are certain similarities between a human embryo and certain lower forms of life, but since most animals are somewhat similar in basic structure, being made of cells, and also in basic function, needing nutriment, oxygen, and a way to dispose of waste materials, it is only natural that in the course of its development the human embryo should resemble some lower animals. What its ancestors were has nothing to do with these resemblances.

In fact, the actual resemblances are usually quite superficial. The famous "gill slits," which were almost always used by evolutionists to prove this argument, only illustrate this. The embryo when a month old has certain folds on what is becoming its neck that could perhaps be imagined to resemble the gills of a fish. Any resemblance is, however, very superficial, as the folds never have the function or the material of gills and gradually develop into jaw, neck, etc. The gill slit argument offers about as much proof that man evolved from the fish as the moon-shaped face of a young Chinese is proof that he evolved from the moon.

Vestigial Organs

Evolution's argument with regard to rudimental or vestigial organs is that the existence of certain organs which have no function shows that they are evolutionary leftovers, that is, organs which did have a function somewhere down the evolutionary line, but which are no longer useful to the organism, though still present in it.

According to evolutionists today, evolution came about by means of mutations, which are small, completely accidental changes. Evolutionists hold that there was no plan of a creator to direct its course.

If the multitude of organs which we now have

19

came about in this way by evolutionary process, it seems that we should find many unnecessary organs which do no good to the organism, but which do no harm either, not only organs which functioned in a lower animal, but also other organs which could eventually evolve into something helpful or disappear altogether. For example, with as many really useful bones as we have, it seems that there should be one here and there which does nothing, but hurts nothing. Or why should there be just two eyes in front of the head? Couldn't an eye just as easily have grown under the skin in a location where it does neither good nor harm, were it all by accident?

Organs which at one stage in our evolution functioned but are needed no more should certainly be found. Also if evolution is continuing, there should be things which do little or nothing now, but will in the ages to come develop into organs as yet unknown. Searching for these vestigial organs, past generations of scientists have found in humans about one hundred eighty organs with no known function. Some of these are more highly developed in lower animals.

These few organs were once greatly used as evidence for evolution. However, with the progress of science, it was discovered that many of them were glands which produced very necessary hormones. Others were found to function in the embryonic stage, and some functioned only as a reserve, when other organs were destroyed. Of the few which were left, others functioned only in periods of emergency. Those organs which would be claimed to be vestigial today are very few and an ever-growing number of scientists feel that there are none at all—that is, that these few organs for which uses have not yet been found probably have uses which will one day be discovered.

The small number of organs considered by anyone as vestigial today constitute a strong evidence against evolution. There would almost of necessity be many non-functioning organs if all of our organs came about only by chance accidents of mutation. In addition, a few vestigial organs could never constitute proof against God's creation. His creation allows for mutations of the type which have actually been observed, which are almost all degenerative, and which could easily account for some organs not being functional now which once were. Since the theory of evolution demands many useless developing or degenerating organs, and science has now proved them not to exist, they have become an important evidence against evolution, and should not be just quietly dropped from the books.

The Appendix

The vestigial organ which has been most commonly used to prove evolution is the appendix. In "less evolved" animals the appendix is larger than that of man, and in some it has a clear function. It is stated that man, evolving from hypothetical ancestors with larger, functioning appendixes, kept his appendix but lost its functions. There are, however, animals considered less evolved than those having functioning appendixes which have smaller nonfunctioning appendixes than that of man, and other animals which have no appendixes. If we are honest in using the appendix as a proof that man is more evolved than the animals which have more highly developed functioning appendixes, we are forced to acknowledge that it proves that man is less evolved than the animals in which the appendix is less developed or even absent. Furthermore, it could just as easily be said that these animals evolved from man. According to *Encyclopedia Britannica*, "Animals that have the same organ in a fully developed and functional condition are believed to be close to the ancestry of the animals having the vestigial organ."[5] This makes man close in ancestry to the

5. Vol. 1, p. 983.

marsupials and rabbits in which the appendix is well developed, and distant from the monkeys which generally do not have appendixes. Other scientists feel that the appendix is not vestigial at all, but that it has a function which is not yet clear.

Man's next most frequently cited vestigial organs are his scalp and ear muscles. These are more highly developed in the horse, for example, and are used to disturb flies that land on his head. The argument is that man can use his hands for shooing flies and does not need scalp and ear muscles. Therefore they are vestigial. I take this as a personal insult, for I can easily move my scalp and ears and often twitch them to keep off flies. If the people who use this argument have degenerated muscles, they must be very seriously inconvenienced indeed, having to stop what they are doing for every fly that comes by, and will probably eventually be eliminated in their struggle for the survival of the fittest.

Instead of proving evolution, the smallness of the number of organs whose uses are not known is a strong proof that they did not come into being through accidental mutations and the fact that it is still cited at all simply demonstrates the paucity of the evidence for evolution.

Fossils

Darwin, in *The Origin of Species* wrote,

But just in proportion as this process of extermination has acted on an enormous scale, so must the number of intermediate varieties, which have formerly existed, be truly enormous. Why then is not every geological formation and every stratum full of such intermediate links? Geology assuredly does not reveal any such finely-graduated organic chain; and this, perhaps, is the most obvious and serious objection which can be urged against the theory. The explanation lies, as I believe, in the extreme imperfection of the geological record.[6]

The problem of the fossil record is still with us. The missing links are still missing.

The following quotation from an article by Duane T. Gish clarifies the problem the fossil record presents to the evolutionist. He has presented a basic outline of creation and of evolution, and then goes on to examine the predictions which could be made about the fossil record on a basis of these two models.

Creation model	Evolution model
Sudden appearance in great variety of highly complex forms	Gradual change of simplest forms into more and more complex forms
Sudden appearance of each created kind with ordinal characteristics complete. Sharp boundaries separating major taxonomic groups. No transitional forms between higher categories	Transitional series linking all categories. No systematic gaps

Let us now compare the known facts of the fossil record with the predictions of the two models.

Advent of Life in the Cambrian

The oldest rocks in which indisputable fossils are found are those of the Cambrian Period. In

---

6. Charles Darwin, *The Origin of Species*, First Collier Books Edition, p. 308.

these sedimentary deposits are found billions and billions of fossils of highly complex forms of life. These include sponges, corals, jellyfish, worms, mollusks, and crustaceans; in fact, every one of the major invertebrate forms of life has been found in Cambrian rocks. These animals were so highly complex that, it is conservatively estimated, they would have required 1.5 billion years to evolve.

What do we find in rocks older than the Cambrian? Not a single, indisputable multicellular fossil has ever been found in Precambrian rocks. Certainly it can be said without fear of contradiction that the evolutionary ancestors of the Cambrian fauna, if they ever existed, have never been found (Simpson, 1960, p. 143; Cloud, 1968; Alexrod, 1958).

Concerning this problem, Axelrod (1958) has stated, "One of the major unsolved problems of geology and evolution is the occurrence of diversified, multicellular marine invertebrates in Lower Cambrian rocks on all the continents and their absence in rocks of greater age." After discussing the varied types that are found in the Cambrian, Axelrod goes on to say, "However, when we turn to examine the Precambrian rocks for the forerunners of these Early Cambrian fossils they are nowhere to be found. Many thick (over 5,000 feet) sections of sedimentary rock are now known to lie in unbroken succession below strata containing the earliest Cambrian fossils. These sediments apparently were suitable for the preservation of fossils because they are often identical with overlying rocks which are fossiliferous, yet no fossils are found in them."

From all appearances, then, based on the known facts of historical record, there occurred a sudden great outburst of life at a high level of complexity. The fossil record gives no evidence that these Cambrian animals were derived from preceding, ancestral forms. Furthermore, not a

24

single fossil has been found that can be considered to be a transitional form between the major groups, or phyla. At their earliest appearance these major invertebrate types were just as clearly and distinctly set apart as they are today.

How do these facts compare with the predictions of the evolution model? They are in clear contradiction to such predictions. This has been admitted, for instance by George (1960, p. 5), who states, "Granted an evolutionary origin of the main groups of animals and not an act of special creation, the absence of any record whatsoever of a single member of any of the phyla in the Precambrian rocks remains as inexplicable on orthodox grounds as it was to Darwin." Simpson has struggled valiantly but not fruitfully with this problem and has been forced to concede (1949, p. 18) that the absence of Precambrian fossils (other than alleged fossil microorganisms) is the "major mystery of the history of life."

These facts, however, are in full agreement with the predictions of the creation model. The fossil record *does* reveal (i) a sudden appearance, in great variety, of highly complex forms with no evolutionary ancestors and (ii) the absence of transitional forms between the major taxonomic groups, just as postulated on the basis of creation. Most emphatically, the known facts of the fossil record from the very outset support the predictions of the creation model but unquestionably contradict the predictions of the evolution model.

Discrete Nature of Vertebrate Classes

The remainder of the history of life reveals a remarkable absence of the many transitional forms demanded by the theory. There is, in fact, a *systematic* deficiency of transitional forms between the higher categories, just as predicted by the creation model.

25

The idea that the vertebrates are derived from the invertebrates is purely an assumption that cannot be documented from the fossil record. In the history of the study of the comparative anatomy and embryology of living forms almost every invertebrate group has been proposed, at one time or another, as the ancestor of the vertebrates (E. G. Conklin, as quoted in Allen, 1969; Romer, 1966, p. 12). The transition from invertebrate to vertebrate supposedly passed through a simple chordate stage. Does the fossil record provide evidence for such a transition? Not at all. Ommaney (1964) has stated, "How this earliest chordate stock evolved, what stages of development it went through to eventually give rise to truly fishlike creatures we do not know. Between the Cambrian when it probably originated, and the Ordovician when the first fossils of animals with really fishlike characteristics appeared, there is a gap of perhaps 100 million years which we will probably never be able to fill."

Incredible! 100 million years of evolution and no transitional forms! All hypotheses combined, no matter how ingeniously, could never pretend, on the basis of evolution theory, to account for a gap of such magnitude. Such facts, on the other hand, are in perfect accord with the predictions of the creation model. . . .

The examples cited in this paper are in no way exceptional; rather, they serve to illustrate what is characteristic of the fossil record. Although transitions at the subspecies level are observable and those at the species level may be inferred, the absence of transitional forms between higher categories (the created kinds of the creation model) is regular and systematic.[7]

7. Duane T. Gish, "Creation, Evolution, and the Historical Evidence," *The American Biology Teacher,* March 1973, pp. 135-138. For a more complete treatment, see: Duane T. Gish, *Evolution?—The Fossils Say No!,* Institute for Creation Research, 1972.

There are a few classic examples which are used very often, which give the student the impression that the connecting links have really been found. Perhaps best known is the archaeopteryx. The archaeopteryx is a long-extinct creature with some birdlike features, such as feathers and ability to fly; some reptilelike features, such as a kind of finger arrangement on the wing joint, and teeth. While it can be explained as a stage through which birds passed while evolving from reptiles, it could also have been simply a distinct curious creature like the bat, which is a mammal with ability to fly, fingers on the wing joints, and teeth. The bat is never considered a link in the evolution of mammals from birds because evolutionists do not think mammals evolved from birds; but the relationship is much the same!

In our time many animals have become extinct, and the number of living species becomes ever smaller. The archaeopteryx, which could be accounted for as an evolutionary link, could also be simply an extinct bird, as evidently there were formerly more types of life in existence than at present.

Some textbooks may categorically present one group or another as the ancestor of almost any animal, giving the impression that they know what the various animals have evolved from. Davidheiser, however, has shown how uncertain evolution really is by quoting its own authorities. I have chosen to reproduce only the mammals from Davidheiser's impressive and well-documented list, since their evolution should be relatively more recent, and the ancestry more certain.

Mammals. "The first successful true mammals . . . were small insectivore types whose relationship to these reptiles is not at all clear."
The monotremes, or egg-laying mammals. "Their geologic history is completely unknown."
The marsupials, or pouched mammals. "Their

origin is extremely ancient and its sources are not known. . . ."

The numbat, or banded anteater. "No bigger than a large brown rat, this banded ant-eater . . . has an origin which, in its exact details, is shrouded in mystery."

The Eutheria, or placental mammals. "From some unknown, primitive, tree-living, insect-eating, and pouched animals there soon arose the earliest placental mammals."

The rodents. " . . . the question of their origin must be left open."

The lagomorphs (rabbits and hares). (They formerly were considered to be rodents, but now are thought to be not even related to the rodents.) "The origin of these animals is uncertain."

The elephants. "The two survivors of the great Order Proboscidia are *Elephas maximus* of Asia and *Laxodonta africana* of Africa. The origins of both are obscure. . . ."

The sea cows. "Their origin is still a mystery to men of science. . . ."

The Aardvark. "Their prehistoric record is, however, fragmentary and offers little evidence as to their immediate ancestors."

The Pinnipedia (seals, sea lions, walruses). " . . . the progenitors of the pinnipeds are completely unknown. . . ."

The cetaceans, the whales and porpoises. "Agorophilus exhibits slightly more primitive features but does not furnish any clue to the affinities of whales with any known terrestrial mammalian order."

The Mystacoceti, or baleen whales. "The origin of the Mystacoceti is uncertain."

The Artiodactyla, or even-toed hoofed animals. " . . . their origin is uncertain."

The hippopotamus. " . . . their pedigree is uncertain."

The Perissodactyla, or odd-toed hoofed animals. "The Perissodactyla as an order probably originated in the northern hemisphere . . . from some as yet undiscovered relatives of the Eocene condylarths or protoungulates."

Horses. "The real origin of horses is unknown."

The Primates. This includes lemurs, monkeys, apes, and man. "When and where the first Primates made their appearance is also conjectural. . . . It is clear then that the earliest Primates are not yet known. . . ."

The tarsier. "The evolutionary origin of these tarsiers is still in some doubt."

Monkeys of the Western Hemisphere. "The phylogenetic history of the New World monkeys or platyrrhines is quite unknown."

Monkeys of the Eastern Hemisphere. "As to the Old World monkeys, even less is known of their past. But they too must go back to unknown Eocene ancestors. . . ."

The gibbon. "Its origin has not yet been traced."

Man. ". . . there is still no general agreement as to where true *Homo sapiens*, the men of our own species, developed. Each authority has his own theory for which he will fight like a mother for her child."

Neanderthal man. "Their true place in the evolution of man has never been established."

Cro-Magnon man. "Cro-Magnon man is a modern man in every sense of the word, but where he came from or how he came about we have not the slightest idea."

The Negritos. "It was thought at one time that they represent an earlier stage in the evolution of man, but there is no fossil evidence that man went through a pygmy stage. . . ."

And finally, in conclusion, *EVERYTHING!* "We do not actually know the phylogenetic history of any group of plants and animals since it lies in the undecipherable past."[8]

---

8. Bolton Davidheiser, *Evolution and Christian Faith*, 1969, pp. 307-309.

To summarize this line of evidence, the fossils show rather distinct groups which, though showing some variation, do not seem to have enough similarity to indicate clearly evolution from one group to another. Although the evolutionist tries to bridge these gaps by suggesting unknown ancestors for almost all groups, the evidence would seem to show instead that the various groups were created distinctly, though with a capacity for a limited amount of variation.

Darwin considered the fossil record to be the most serious objection against his theory, and this objection still stands today. However, most evolutionists of today also see in fossils most important evidence for their cause. Simply stated, they maintain that older rocks contain fossils of animals which are more simple; whereas, younger rocks contain fossils of animals which are more complex.

This idea naturally brings up the question, "How does one know which rocks are the oldest?" Geologists base their determinations of the age of rocks on the fossils which are found in them. Those which contain fossils of simpler animals are considered older, and those which contain fossils of more complex animals are considered younger. With a system like this it would seem that they couldn't miss, and one could cite almost any geologist to show that this is the principal method used to date strata. Professor R. A. Stirton, Director of the Museum of Paleontology at the University of California in Berkeley, puts this idea very clearly, "Biologic correlations are still the most useful method in our efforts to establish relative contemporaneity of events throughout the geologic past. They are based on the history of life as represented by fossils in the rocks."[9] Where the fossils in one part of a stratum of rock are different from those in another part of the same layer, they generally go by the fossils rather than the fact that it all seems to

9. *Time, Life, and Man*, 1959, p. 83.

be one layer, laid down at the same time. We see then that the fossils are used to determine the age of the rocks which contain them. The simplest fossils therefore cannot help being in the rocks which are considered older, and the more complex in rocks which are younger.

Here we find our first problem. In most mountainous regions on every continent there are many examples of strata with fossils where the less complex are on top of more complex fossils.[10] It would be natural to think that the strata on top are more recent than those underneath, but when they contain fossils which are "less evolved" they are called older. The problem of how rocks laid down earlier could climb on top of rocks laid down later is so serious for the evolutionists, that to resolve it, they say that the rocks on top did not form there by sedimentation but came from some other place. This is possible in the case of actual thrust faults which are relatively small amounts of rock which have been pushed up over older layers, but in many cases countless millions of tons of rock would have to have moved, sometimes for hundreds of miles, to find themselves on top of "more recent" strata. Even this might occasionally be possible if we were dealing with broken and twisted layers, but it is often smooth, even strata—in many cases thousands of square miles in area—many parts of which show no signs of wear or breakage from the trip, but from all evidence seem to have been formed in place.

Let's take the Lewis Overthrust for an example. It is 6 miles thick and 135 to 350 miles long. One sees at a glance how difficult it must be for the uniformitarian geologists to believe that it slid the 35 to 40 miles which they feel must have been necessary to arrive in its present place—but that is what they say.

10. John C. Whitcomb and Henry M. Morris: *The Genesis Flood*, 1962, p. 180. See also *The Bulletin of the Geological Society of America*, Vol. 70, Feb. 1959, pp. 115-122.

A number of theories have been presented which seek to explain how this movement of the stone could have come about. Some of these could have worked if the amount of rock had been small. One important theory advanced is that gravity moved the rock from a higher position to a lower one. This conjecture, however, fails to explain how the huge masses of rock many square miles in area, including entire mountains and valleys, could have slid. Neither does it explain the lack of any signs of movement. Although it is a disturbed area, there is nothing that resembles evidence of this kind of movement.[11] In addition, if we imagine that the level of the top of the rocks on which the Lewis Overthrust now rests was at sea level and that the overthrust rested beside it, the top of the overthrust would have had to extend 31,580 feet into the sky. This would have made it more than 2,000 feet higher than Mount Everest, presently the highest point on the earth's surface, which towers 29,028 feet into the air. But that is not all. In order for it to be enough higher to be able to slide downhill thirty-five to forty miles, the Lewis Overthrust would have to have been so high as to be beyond the range of credibility. If instead the land sank ahead of it, the problem would seem to be compounded. Not many teachers clutter their students' minds with this side of the picture of evolution for it would then be most difficult for them to accept much of the fossil evidence with the blind faith it requires if one is to accept the age and significance claimed for it.

Many of the mountains of the Alps are said to have moved, the Matterhorn having traveled from twenty to one hundred miles, depending on whose authority one accepts. Let me quote the eloquent description of F. C. Lane in the *Encyclopedia Americana.* "In this global commotion the Matterhorn, a gigantic

---

11. Whitcomb and Morris: *Genesis Flood*, pp. 184-200.

splinter, seems to have been caught up like a bit of flotsam and removed bodily some twenty miles or more."[12] The Mythen, another peak now found in the Alps, is said to have made the journey all the way from Africa. Would it not be simpler to assume that these examples were deposited where they are, and that the simpler fossils are found above the more complex ones because they lived later, and that the more complex ones did not evolve from the simpler ones at all?

All of this brings us to another problem. Geologists of the evolutionist persuasion hold to the uniformitarian school of thought. Webster defines this as follows: "A geological doctrine that existing processes acting in the same manner and with essentially the same intensity as at present are sufficient to account for all geological changes."[13]

As has been seen, in practice evolutionists make exceptions when a uniformitarian explanation would disprove evolution, but in general uniformitarianism is necessary to the theory of evolution. One reason is that the long periods of time necessary to build everything up by today's methods is a necessity to the shaky foundation of the theory of evolution. That a flood as described in the Bible in the time of Noah could deposit as much material in a year as would normally be laid down in many years would be unacceptable to evolutionists because, as will be shown, a fantastically longer period of time would be necessary for evolution to be a statistical possibility than can possibly be arrived at by any method of dating. Because of this, every additional year that evolutionists can find is a help to the theory. This is not to say that if there were sufficient time evolution

---

12. Vol. 1, 1958, p. 440.
13. Webster's *Third New International Dictionary* (unabridged), 1964, p. 2498.

could have accomplished what its supporters say, but simply to point out their recognition that without a fantastically long period to work in, evolution just isn't feasible. Obviously God could as easily have created five billion years ago as yesterday, so the length of time is no problem one way or the other to the creationist, except for the following exception: Biblical views of creation can be divided into two general groups. One interprets the six days of creation mentioned in Genesis 1 to refer to six literal days, and the other considers the creation period to refer to six ages or pictures of God's creation. Those who feel that the account speaks of twenty-four-hour days usually feel that the earth could not be as old as evolutionists believe it to be. Arguments for a recent creation, such as the one given above, will be mentioned where applicable, but it must be remembered that though a short age for the world would exclude the possibility of man's having developed by evolution from a single cell, showing the world to be older would prove neither evolution to be true nor the Bible to be false.

Everyone, whether creationist or evolutionist, relies to some extent on what he knows of the present to interpret the past. There is, however, good evidence that not everything in the past took place in the same way, and at the same rate as today. When an event did not happen in the same way as it happens today, trying to understand it as if it had to gain extra years for evolution can only lead to confusion. The creationist recognizes this as he insists on a moment of creation instead of an ever-continuing evolution, and as he believes in a Biblical flood. The evolutionist also recognizes it, whether he wants to admit it or not, as he insists on mountains sliding for miles in a way which could not happen now. Either one must be taken on faith with no present day counterpart.

I am sorry, but it is awfully hard to become a fossil anymore. To be fossilized, you must be preserved in some way from the decomposition which starts immediately after death and continues until an organism is completely decomposed.

A glance at the methods by which fossils have been preserved is enough to show that there have been some changes in the circumstances which don't go well with the uniformitarian viewpoint of geology.

In Siberia the remains of many millions of animals have been found frozen in the muck. Among these have been some which were frozen so rapidly that the hair and even the flesh has been preserved. A great part of the flesh of some specimens was in good enough condition for sledge dogs to eat and enjoy.[14] This rapid freezing and staying frozen is hard to explain by conditions observed today.

Another type of fossilization is the preservation of bones, teeth, and other hard parts. This happens when animals become trapped in sediment and water. It happens every once in a while now. It is difficult however, by today's processes to explain the great cemeteries of fossils found here and there throughout the world. There are areas of millions of fossils piled one on top of another, sometimes preserved in positions indicating that they were trapped in their death struggle. Sometimes these are fish, sometimes mammals, and sometimes mixtures. It takes some type of cataclysm to explain this, and if one refuses to accept the flood that the Bible tells about, he must imagine some other drastic cataclysm.

Carbonization is another means of forming fossils. Our coal deposits are the result of this process. Coal

---

14. *Encyclopedia Americana*, 1950, Vol. 18, p. 180.

was formed from decomposed plant life under great pressure.

Petrification, another mode of forming fossils, requires that that which petrifies be entirely underground where minerals and water can work on it before the material decomposes. The noted evolutionist L. S. B. Leakey, writing of a beetle, caterpillars, and other insects perfectly turned to stone asks, "How did these incredible fossils occur? We simply do not know."[15]

We see, then, that evolution finds itself hard pressed to explain the existence of many of the fossils on which proof of the theory is laid, without abandoning the uniformitarian view of geology which evolutionists feel must be retained insofar as possible to allow time enough for evolution to work.

Radioactive Dating

Much honor is given today to the dates which have been determined by utilizing that which science knows of the rate of decomposition of radioactive materials. Many times enthusiastic authors in writing for the general public give the impression that this method has placed beyond question the dates which they have established.

For example, L. S. B. Leakey in writing of his famous discovery of a fossil which at that time he considered human and named *Zinjanthropus* stated: "Now, at last, we have the facts—and they are truly staggering. A dating method known as the potassium-argon process places *Zinjanthropus* not merely hundreds of thousands of years, but an almost incredible 1,750,000 years in the past."[16]

In more advanced geologic texts, however, we look in vain for this positiveness. Instead, after discussing

---

15. "Adventures in the Search for Man," *National Geographic*, January 1963, p. 149.

16. *National Geographic*, Vol. 120, No. 4, October 1961.

the methods and problems of radioactive dating, A. O. Woodford concludes, and the majority of evolutionists agree: "At present, fossil correlations seem to be safer guides in most cases."[17] In practice the radioactive dates which evolutionary geologists accept are those which do not conflict with fossil dating.

Why does certainty of the radiometric dating evaporate when authorities are writing for an audience of geologists? A closer look at this method of dating will explain. First of all, whether the radioactive material be carbon, potassium, uranium, or some other substance, the general method is the same. The substance which breaks down by shooting off atomic particles must be accurately measured, and the products of this breakdown must be accurately measured. Then by knowing the rate of disintegration and assuming it to have been constant throughout the ages, calculations can be made to determine the age. It is much like determining how long a candle has been burning by measuring what is left of the candle, and calculating the rate at which it presently burns. If the candle has always burned at that speed, and you guess right as to its original length, you can be quite accurate. You can never know for sure, however, that these assumptions of speed and original length were correct.[18]

With the exception of the carbon 14 method of radioactive dating, the fossils in question cannot themselves be dated, but only the strata in which they are found. This is further complicated by the fact that the sedimentary rocks which contain fossils cannot actually be dated either. Dates must be calculated by finding igneous layers containing the proper radioactive materials, and trying to correlate their ages with those of the sedimentary strata in question by their position above, below, etc.

---

17. Woodford, *Historical Geography*, p. 218.
18. Donald E. Chittick: *Creation, Evolution, and the Scripture*, 1966, p. 79.

Another major problem is that the original element and the product of radiation have differing degrees of solubility in the various mineral solutions contained in ground water, and it is impossible to be sure how much of each has been carried away during the ages, a problem which is fantastically compounded if one accepts the millions of years which are generally presented. In addition, however, there is also a problem of one or the other elements being washed in from elsewhere to further reduce the method's accuracy.

The result is that, of the many ages which have been determined by the method, most have been rejected by the geologists themselves, with the exception of C-14 dates which are somewhat better accepted.

The date of the Leakey skull mentioned above, was determined by one of the most important of the radioactive dating methods, that of the disintegration of potassium. The product of the decay of potassium which the scientists measure is argon. The whole conclusion is worthless if any of either the potassium, which is one of the most active elements, or the argon, a gas, has been leached out or has escaped from the rock during a period that they feel has been millions of years.

Even being sure of accurate measurements is not easy. In the case of the argon, the sample must be freed of argon contained in the air by heating, etc., and then further heated to release the argon formed in the sample which is then absorbed in charcoal which hopefully had no other argon in it.

The importance of radioactive dating to the theory of evolution stems from the fact that this method of dating generally produces very old dates, usually putting the age of the earth at from three to five billion years.

This is only a drop in the bucket to what would have been necessary had living things actually developed by evolution, as no amount of time is sufficient to produce men from chance variations, but psychologically it is certainly a help. If the earth is actually that old it is no proof that God did not make it and the things in it. If it is not that old, this fact would constitute a good evidence against evolution. At best, radioactive dates are shaky because they depend on assumptions that no one can prove: that the rate of disintegration has never changed, that there was none of the daughter product of the radiation present at the beginning, and that nothing has happened in the intervening years to destroy the accuracy of the measurements.

Dating by Ocean Salt and Sediment and Meteoric Dust

At this point another method of calculating the age of the earth enters in. Scientists have found that assuming the ocean to have started out with no salt at all, and never to have received salt at a more rapid rate than at present, it could not be more than 200,000 years old and probably not more than 50,000 years old. There is no reason to believe the first assumption, that it started out with no salt at all, and the second is obviously false, as salt is readily soluble, and would of course have been dissolved and deposited at a much more rapid rate if the ocean did not start out salty, because the percentage in the continents would have to have been much higher.

All of this points to a very recent creation. Evolutionary scientists have long recognized this problem, but have accepted the dates suggested by radioactivity instead of that suggested by the salt in the ocean because the radioactive dates better supported their theory. Some scientists, trying to harmonize the problem, have suggested a salt cycle. A little salt, of course, would be redeposited on the continents by animals, etc., but their idea is that the ocean is no saltier than it is because the salt by some as yet unknown method flows back into the continents from the ocean to be carried again to the ocean. Giving them the benefit of the doubt (using the oldest possible age which they feel the salt method could possibly attribute to the ocean, and the youngest radioactive dates they feel the earth could possibly have) the radioactive age of the earth is at least twenty times that of the salt age. The salt would therefore have to have made its complete cycle through the continents at least twenty times. To believe this, one would have to believe that while the salt was passing through the continents at least twenty times, the materials used in radioactive dating could not have moved the few feet necessary to ruin their dating accuracy!

Another evidence for a recent creation comes from studies begun in 1968 of cores taken from the bottoms of the seas. "Sediment formed by microscopic marine organisms and dust blown or washed into the sea should have blanketed the ocean beds over the ages to a uniform depth of at least twelve miles. Yet there is practically no sediment in the center of the Atlantic and only a half-mile veneer near the borders."[19] Just exactly what age this would augur for the sea is difficult to calculate at this point, but it would obviously not be enough time for evolution as it is conceived by evolutionists today to have taken place. The new theory that the earth's surface is composed of large moving plates provides a hiding place for some of this sediment, but at this writing it appears doubtful that it will provide a complete explanation.

Meteoric dust presents the same sort of difficulty to those whose theory requires a very old date for the earth. "At the rate at which meteoric dust is falling

19. Ronald Schiller, "The Continents Are Adrift!" *Reader's Digest*, April 1971, p. 103.

and settling on the earth, a layer of this dust fifty-four feet deep should have been built up since the time it is estimated by the scientists on other grounds that the earth had a solid crust. Mixing with the surface materials cannot account for the absence of this dust. Meteoric dust is very rich in nickel, and to account for the nickel of meteoric dust mixing with the earth's surface (assuming no nickel present originally) would require a mixing to a depth of more than three miles."[20] It is estimated that over 1000 tons of meteroic dust falls to earth each day.[21]

Radiocarbon Dating

While subject to some of the same problems as other radioactive dating methods, radiocarbon dating is important for dating human fossils, because it dates more recent times. The carbon 14 isotope, which is radioactive, is introduced into the air about five or six miles up, when cosmic rays collide with nitrogen of the air. The radioactive carbon formed reacts with the oxygen of the air to form carbon dioxide which is absorbed by plants, and so passes also to the animals which eat them. When a plant or animal dies, it ceases to take in new carbon dioxide, and the carbon 14 taken in previously disintegrates at a constant rate of one-half of the total amount every 5568 years. (The Fifth Radiocarbon Dating Conference in 1962 said 5730 years instead.) The amounts of radiocarbon already existing on earth, most of which is in the sea, and the average rate of its production must be assumed to have remained constant for the 20,000 to 60,000 years or so for which scientists feel that this method of dating is accurate. W. F. Libby, the father of radiocarbon dating and its foremost authority, says that radiocarbon dates agree well with historical dates

20. Davidheiser, *Evolution and Christian Faith*, p. 298.
21. D. W. R. McKinley, "Meteor," *Encyclopedia Britannica*, 1965, Vol. 15, p. 270.

back to 4000 years ago. For non-Egyptian dates "the uncertainty in the historical ages of the individual samples and the scatter beyond 4000 years ago are large."[22] As to the agreement between Egyptian historical dates and radiocarbon dates, "The two sets of dates agree back to 4000 years ago."[23] Dr. Libby feels that the greater differences for earlier dates is due to the inaccuracy of the earlier historic dates, though it could also be from inaccuracy of the carbon dates due to more or less cosmic wave activity and a number of other factors too complicated to discuss here.

Since evolutionary concepts would demand that the earth be very old, it is assumed that the amount of radiocarbon in the atmosphere remains constant because an equilibrium has long since been achieved between its rate of formation and its rate of decomposition. The fact is however, that the rate of formation is 2.5 atoms per square centimeter per second, and the rate of decomposition is 1.9 atoms per square centimeter per second. Libby accounts for the difference by the radiocarbon which is irretrievably deposited in the bottom of the seas.

Prof. M. A. Cook, chemist and winner of the Nitro Nobel gold medal, points out that this would mean that sediments would have to have accumulated from 135 to 200 times faster than uniformitarian geologists had thought, and that either evolution is compressed from 600 million years to a maximum of 4.4 million years, or else an equilibrium has not yet been reached, which would infer an even more recent creation. In neither case would there have been enough time for evolution to have taken place in any way that would fit at all into present evolutionary theories. An alternate to Libby's explanation, that in-

22. "Accuracy of Radiocarbon Dates," Science, Vol. 140, April 19, 1963, p. 278.
23. Ibid.

stead of being irretrievably deposited the carbon in sea bottom sediments is. somehow recirculated, has virtually the same problem, and would also mean that radiocarbon dates have been too old.[24]

The dates which have been established by radio-carbon dating have been published in *Science* up through 1959, and in the *Radiocarbon* annual there-after. In looking through these dates, one is at first struck by the fact that the overwhelming majority of samples dated are quite recent, with a rather small percentage having over ten thousand years.

R. L. Whitelaw, Professor of Nuclear and Mechanical Engineering, Virginia Polytechnic, has gone on to analyze the fifteen thousand dates that have been determined in the thirty years that this method of dating has been in use. He assumes that if the vast eons of time postulated by evolution are correct, such a world-wide random sampling should yield twenty thousand specimens which are undatable (because the radioactive carbon would already be broken down) for each datable specimen. Perhaps decomposition of the very old, and a certain interest in studying archeo-logical specimens which are more recent would cut this ratio down somewhat, but his findings are still impressive. Checking out all dates up to the end of 1969, he has found only a tiny minority to be un-datable by radiocarbon dating methods. Just three (some megapod eggs) out of the fifteen thousand dates are called "infinite" and a few others over fifty thousand years! All prehistoric human remains and artifacts that have been dated have been assigned ages within sixty thousand years.[25]

---

24. "Carbon-14 and the Age of the Atmosphere," *Creation Research Society Quarterly*, Vol. 7, June 1970, pp. 53-56.

25. "Time, Life and History in the Light of 15,000 Radio-carbon Dates," *Creation Research Society Quarterly*, Vol. 7, June 1970, p. 56.

Since the evolutionists establish the age of the strata by the fossils that are found in them, it would seem that the fossils should go well with the ages assigned to the rocks in which they are found. Often, however, they don't.

When, instead of in a progression from simple to complex, fossils are found together of such various degrees of complexity that according to the theory, they should not have been living at the same time, it shows that fossil evidence does not always support the evolutionary ideas as it is made to appear to do.

One of the most interesting examples of fossils getting out of step with their strata is the case of the apparently human footprints. These are of sufficient importance to merit the following long quotation from Henry M. Morris, who for a time served as head of the civil engineering department of Virginia Polytechnic Institute:

> For example, there is the case of the human footprints that have frequently been found in supposedly very ancient strata. Man, of course, is supposed to have evolved only in the late Tertiary, at the earliest, and therefore to be only about one million years old. But what appear to be human footprints have been found in rocks from as early as the Carboniferous Period, supposedly some 250,000,000 years old. Says Ingalls:
>
>> On sites reaching from Virginia and Pennsylvania, through Kentucky, Illinois, Missouri and westward toward the Rocky Mountains, prints similar to those shown above [referring to several accompanying pictures] and from 5 to 10 inches long, have been found on the surface of exposed rocks, and more and more keep turning up as the years go by.
>
> These prints give every evidence of having been made by human feet, at a time when the rocks

were soft mud. As indicated in the quotation, this sort of thing is not a rare occurrence but is found rather frequently. However, geologists refuse to accept the evidence at face value, because it would mean either that modern man lived in the earliest years of the postulated evolutionary history or that his history must be condensed to a duration measured by the history of man. Neither alternative is acceptable. Ingalls says:

> If man, or even his ape ancestor, or even that ape ancestor's early mammalian ancestor, existed as far back as in the Carboniferous Period in any shape, then the whole science of geology is so completely wrong that all the geologists will resign their jobs and take up truck driving. Hence for the present at least, science rejects the attractive explanation that man made these mysterious prints in the mud of the Carboniferous Period with his feet.[26]

Since these strata are, according to the evolutionists, around 250 times older than man could possibly be, it is clear that they pose quite a problem. According to A. C. Ingalls, scientists whose presuppositions will not allow them to accept these as human footprints are divided between two possible solutions as to their origin: (1) That they were carved by ancient Indians; (2) That they were formed by some now unknown animal, which left footprints resembling those of human beings.[27]

Another proof which is similar but more interesting is found at the Paluxy River near Glen Rose, Texas. The river exposed, in stratum supposed to be from the Cretaceous Period, tracks of both people and dinosaurs. According to the evolutionary theory, man did not evolve until seventy million years after

26. Whitcomb and Morris, *Genesis Flood*, pp. 172-173.
27. "The Carboniferous Mystery," *Scientific American*, Vol. 162, January 1940, p. 14.

the Cretaceous Period. How, then, could these two sets of prints have been laid down side by side in the same strata? Morris concludes that both were formed after the creation of man, and that the time periods postulated by evolution are seriously exaggerated.

At the opposite extreme as far as this type of fossil evidence is concerned, we find that some animals believed to have been extinct for years and used to date the strata in which they were found, have been found still very much alive today.

These few illustrations serve to point out the fact that there are many problems involved in dating strata. Writing of this, Robin S. Allen, a geologist of some importance, states:

> Because of the sterility of its concepts, historical geology, which includes paleontology and stratigraphy, has become static and unreproductive. Current methods of delimiting intervals of time, which are the fundamental units of historical geology, and of establishing chronology are of dubious validity. Worse than that, the criteria of correlation—the attempt to equate in time, or synchronize the geological history of one area with that of another—are logically vulnerable. The findings of historical geology are suspect because the principles upon which they are based are either inadequate, in which case they should be reformulated, or false, in which case they should be discarded. Most of us refuse to discard or reformulate, and the result is the present deplorable state of our discipline.[28]

Since at the present time animals of every grade of complexity live together on the same earth at the same time, the fact that a certain rock has fossils of a certain grade of progress certainly does not prove that the animal lived in a certain past era. This fact be-

---

28. "Geological Correlation and Paleoecology," *Bulletin of the Geological Society of America*, Vol. 59, January 1948, p. 2.

comes especially obvious when the rock lies under other layers which contain less complex fossils.

Evidence that all kinds of plants and animals have always lived together is important because if this could be proved it would completely wipe out the theory of evolution and very strongly support those who believe that creation took place in six literal days.

This evidence is not, however, a necessity for the creation position. Many creationists feel that God created over a longer period of time, and point to the general agreement (though not completely without exceptions) between the order of creation according to the Bible, and the order of evolution according to the evolutionists.

The following quotation from Robert Van Atta summarizes the viewpoint on the strata problem of some creationists who feel that God created over a longer period of time.

> Considering the bearing of the fossil record upon the subject of the origin and history of life, it is significant to note that in any sequence of stratified rocks thick enough to span a considerable length of time, there is a remarkable parallel between the sequence and the creative acts.[29]

Having had something of a glance at fossils in general and their importance to the evolutionary theory, let us pass on to certain of the most important specific fossils.

What Do the Horses Tell Us?

The Encyclopedia Americana says, "Among the numerous examples of organic evolution that of the horse is perhaps more frequently cited and discussed

29. Robert Van Atta, "The Significance of Fossils and Stratigraphy," *Creation, Evolution, and the Scripture*, 1966, pp. 132-133.

than any other."[30] The account then states that the
horse is the animal whose fossil remains demonstrate
more clearly than those of any other animal the
process of evolution, and that this evolution came
about in a regular manner.

Encyclopedia Britannica agrees, saying, "The horse
family has the most complete fossil record of any
group of mammals."[31]

Since the horse provides the best fossil evidence for
evolution, it is important to note what this evidence
does and does not show.

The evidence consists of a number of fossils which
have been lined up in order with those most like the
modern horse, which is supposed to have evolved
consecutively from the ones less like it. These fossils
have not been found deposited one on top of another, with the one with four toes at the bottom, but
dispersed at random throughout the world, making
the determination of any connection between them
very tenuous. There is some disagreement as to
whether these animals should all be considered as
steps in the evolution of the horse, or if some were
separate animals who had nothing to do with the
horse. But if these fossils are correctly placed in the
ancestry of the horse, what does this evidence show?

A difference in the size of the fossils is usually
considered one of the evidences. The eohippus, which
is placed first in line, was smaller than the modern
horse, but the difference in size is usually exaggerated
by comparing the size of the smallest eohippus, which
was the size of a small dog, with modern horses.
Encyclopedia Britannica however states, "Several species of eohippus, ranging in size from a terrier dog to
a Shetland pony, lived in North America and Eu-
rope. . . ."[32] I have found nothing that gives the size

---

30. Vol. 14, p. 390.
31. "Equidae," *Encyclopedia Britannica*, Vol. 8, 1972, p.
658.
32. *Ibid.*, p. 659.

of the smallest modern horse to see how it would compare, but the following quotation gives at least some idea. "A miniature type of pony bred in England often grows no taller than 28 inches."[33] Thus, while the average modern horse is larger than the average eohippus, the difference in size is not too significant when one considers the range in size of modern horses.

The most publicized evidence given for the evolution of the horse is that of the change in the number of its toes. Eohippus had four toes on its front feet and three on its rear instead of just one on each as the modern horse does.

Evolution demands a gradual increase in complexity, which evolutionists say has brought us from the simple cell to life as we have it today. As we will see later, there is no logical method by which evolution in the sense of great increase in complexity could have come about. Because of the impossibility of other ordinary hereditary processes accounting for the variety of life which we see today, most evolutionists agree that it was brought about by mutations. The difficulty here is that observed mutations almost always make organisms more simple (degenerate instead of evolved) if they do not kill them. This is exactly what we see in the horse. Losing toes does not make an organism more complex, but more simple. The process carried to the absolute extreme could reduce the horse to a one-celled animal, but it could not evolve a one-celled animal into a horse.

While this "most frequently cited" of all evidence for evolution does show change, it demonstrates degeneration rather than evolution in complexity. In addition, if the modern horse has come from eohippus, he has lost some teeth in the process and exchanged a stronger arched back for a weaker straight or sway back, both of which seem to be steps in the

---

33. *World Book Encyclopedia*, Vol. 13, 1964, p. 311.

wrong direction. With this kind of evidence for evolution, is it not more simple and more scientific to take by faith that "in the beginning God created...," rather than to take by faith that at some time in the past mutations worked backward from the way they work now? Certainly the evidence of change in the horse from more toes to fewer does not give much basis for the inference of the evolutionists that more complex animals have come from simpler ones.

Human Fossils

Usually when we think of human fossils used as proofs of evolution, we picture in our minds the stooped, hairy half-man, half-ape creatures which we have seen pictured in books, and as statues in museums. In nature they are only found like that in the imagination of the evolutionary artists. It was a newspaper photograph of L. S. B. Leakey[34] which first brought this fact forcefully to my attention. In his fingers he held a tiny piece of bone. It was so small that it was hard to see. He announced in the news story that his find bridged an important gap in the knowledge of the history of human evolution. From tiny pieces such as this evolutionists build big models, not of how the person or animal was, because it is impossible to know this, but of how they would have to have been to fit in with evolutionary theory. This is a serious charge, but I will try to prove it. First, I readily admit that not every case is the same, and that the shape and size of some bones do give artists some help in their drawings; but the number of bones which scientists have is very small. Let us look at some which have been considered most important.

Piltdown man, also called *Eoanthropus dawsoni*, was one of the most important human fossil discoveries. It was found in a gravel pit in Sussex, England,

---

34. *The Oregonian*, Portland, Oregon, March 23, 1962.

in 1912, and was generally used as a strong proof of human evolution in evolutionary books. *Encyclopedia Britannica* called it the second most important of the fossils in showing the evolution of man. From a handful of bones, evolutionary artists built up their models and pictures for museums and textbooks. After many years, Piltdown man was discovered to be a deliberate hoax! The jaw was that of an ape, and the skull modern human, though earlier reports by experts declared it so primitive it was doubted if it had been used in human speech. Both the jaw and the teeth were altered to appear old. One of the small bones of the nose was probably really from some other part of the body of a small animal.

While the Piltdown man does not show evolution, it does show the difficulty, if not the impossibility, of reconstructing with precision a man from the past. Some scientists were skeptical about Piltdown man from the very beginning, as has also been true of most of the other fossil men. However, it was not until forty years later that it was eventually discredited. Today the statues of Piltdown man have been removed from their places in the museums and pictures of him have been eliminated from books, though the harm he has done in destroying people's faith in God's creation of man lives on in the lives of many. It is unfortunate that greater reserve is not used in teaching as facts to school children things recognized by reputable scientists as being questionable.

Another who was once hailed as a progenitor of the human race was the Nebraska man, also called by his more important sounding scientific name *Hesperopithecus*. He was actually nothing more than a tooth, but this was all that was needed by some "experts" to construct the whole man, who naturally looked just like an evolutionist would expect him to. He would probably still be discrediting the Bible if his career had not been finished by the discovery that the tooth belonged to a pig, not to a man.

These illustrations serve to warn us of the strong possibility of error in the interpretation of fossil evidence when one has a preconceived idea into which everything must fit.

The size of the brain case and the sizes and shapes of the other bones are used to determine the degrees of evolution. It must be remembered that such differences also exist among people living today. The bones of today's pygmy, or Australian aborigine, if compared with those of a basketball player, show a great difference, and if placed in the right order could be used to prove either evolution or degeneration to those who did not know that the persons lived at the same time. To show a divergence from modern man, it is really necessary to show the comparison with the most similar modern man, and not just with the average.

There are a number of other difficulties in proving the age of fossil men. One is that people have a habit of burying their dead, instead of leaving them in the strata upon which they lived and walked. This custom could make a tremendous difference if they lived in an eroded area where digging a few feet could put the dead in strata laid down many many years before. Another difficulty, which has already been discussed, is that fossils generally form only under conditions of great pressure, usually under water. Under ordinary conditions existing today bodies decompose. Further compounding the problems is the fact that skeletons are not usually found neatly in order, but in scattered pieces.

Added to the difficulties above is that of dating. Dating in general is very tenuous, being based on the hope of the very evolution it is trying to prove; determining the age of the fossil by the age of its strata, the age of which is in turn determined by the age of the index fossils in it. The difficulty of dating human fossils is even more apparent since for the Pleistocene Period, the period in which geologists think man developed, they have little evidence of evolution of other forms of life, and so lack index fossils. Dating for this period is attempted by climatic changes, with the ice ages being the key to its duration. From one to five ice ages in America have been postulated, with four the number usually mentioned. But uniform agreement is lacking. In addition, evidence from other parts of the world does not do much to support the idea of four ice ages. For example, "Fundamental new studies by A. I. Popov radically change the known facts of the Ice Age in western Siberia. The dominant observable phenomenon of the Quaternary was one extensive marine transgression, not a glaciation."[35]

Evidence strongly suggests, these authors feel, that much of what was considered proof of glaciation was actually a result of seaborn ice. If instead of there being four distinct ice ages the ice erosion occurred during one period only, the Pleistocene Period would be drastically shortened.

The following quote by Frederick Johnson, writing with Willard Libby, the most recognized authority on carbon dating, in defending carbon dating against criticism from proponents of other methods also points out the precariousness of dating this period.

In geology, some, but by no means all, criticisms of the radiocarbon dates are based upon inferences concerning the behavior of a presently non-existent ice sheet. There is no way of proving or disproving assumptions concerning the speed of advance or retreat of the ice, the degree of precision of a varve record and its correlation with the calendar, or the significance of the modifications in the vegetation.[36]

He concludes that it is "absurd" to criticize carbon dates on the basis of this type of evidence. The

35. N. G. Levin, and L. P. Potapov: *The Peoples of Siberia*, 1964, pp. 14-15.
36. Willard F. Libby: *Radiocarbon Dating*, 1955, p. 148.

resulting confusion of dating in a period when man was supposedly evolving is brought out in *Encyclopedia Britannica's* discussion of the last ice age. "It is seen that radiocarbon dating allows only about one-half of the time permitted by the older estimates. . . . The feeling of conservative glacial geologists is that research should be pursued to acquire further and broader information. In the meantime respect is held for carefully documented stratigraphic work and sampling."[37] This means that for now the older dates will be followed instead of the radiocarbon dates which would cut the time in half. As we have already seen, there is good evidence that the radiocarbon dates are themselves too old.

The fossils which evolutionists consider human, or along the evolutionary line toward becoming human, have for years been extremely confusing. The discoverers have each tended to consider his discovery as something unique, of an entirely different type than all the others, sometimes jealously guarding it from the less sympathetic gaze of his fellow scientists. Now, however, a fourfold classification is emerging which we will consider in order of supposed age, taking the oldest first.

Australopithecinae

These are animals similar to gorillas, at least in respect to the bony crest sometimes found on the top of the head, and in the size of their brain. The teeth, however, are somewhat like man's, and it is very probable that they walked erect. Very little else is really known about them, since their fossils are few and fragmentary.

The most well-known *Australopithecines* fossils are *Zinjanthropus* and *Homo habilis*, found by Dr. Leakey in Africa. The most complete of the Leakey

37. R. F. Flint and Morris M. Leighton: "Pleistocene Epoch," *Encyclopedia Britannica*, 1965, Vol. 18, p. 74f.

finds is the major part of a cranium, which when found was in more than four hundred pieces sifted from among tons of earth where they had been scattered. It took more than a year to put them together. One of Leakey's colleagues said it was like reassembling an egg which had been run over by a truck. [38] *Newsweek*, commenting on this and another more recent Leakey find, along with evidence for human evolution in general, states: "The evidence for man's evolution could hardly be more tenuous: a collection of a few hundred fossilized skulls, teeth, jawbones and other fragments. . . . Most anthropologists make no bones about rejecting Leakey's theory. They dismiss hominid No. 3 as Olduval George."[39] (Pun from bones being found in Olduval Gorge.)

In spite of the shape the pieces of skull were in, the skull has not only been reconstructed to evolutionary specifications, but pictures have been shown of how he looked, complete with beard. While reconstructions such as this are usually made with great reservation and reputable scientists warn us as to their limitations, the unfortunate fact remains that they are often used by others to sell evolution to school children without benefit of the reservations and warnings.

Conventional methods of dating placed *Zinjanthropus* in an era over 600,000 years ago. Potassium argon dating of underlying rocks placed it at 1.7 million years.[40]

Most authorities at the time of this revision would put *Australopithecus* out on a limb in drawing man's evolutionary family tree. That is, they would not feel that man evolved from *Australopithecus*, but that both evolved from the same unknown creature.

38. Francis and Datharine: "Earliest Man on Earth?" *Reader's Digest*, January 1964, pp. 157-163.
39. "Bones of Contention," *Newsweek*, February 13, 1967, pp. 101-102.
40. *National Geographic*, 1965, Vol. 127, p. 215.

Homo erectus (Pithecanthropus)

The second group is that of the *Homo erectus*. It is thought to have had some features intermediate between the *Australopithecines* and us, and to have lived a half million years ago.

Among the most important fossils of this group are *Sinanthropus*, also known as *P. pekinensis*—or Peking man, because these fossils were found near Peking in China. The fossils consisted mostly of teeth, lower jaws, and parts of fourteen skulls, which had been broken presumably so that someone or something could eat the brains which supplied about 915 to 1225 cc. of meat apiece. There was with the fossils evidence of the use of fire and tools. All of these fossils were purportedly lost when an attempt was made to take them out of China during the Second World War.

Java man, a skullcap and thighbone, is the other well-known representative of this group. It was first found by Eugene Dubois along with some normal human skulls which he did not mention until thirty years after Java man was well accepted. Later, parts of four other skulls, some teeth, and fragments of lower jaws and thighbones were found. The thighbones are said to be identical to modern man. This gives Java man a very important place in evolution, since the *Homo erectus* head is described by some as apelike. However, since normal human skulls were found as well, there is always the possibility that the legs went with the human skulls instead of going with Java man since they were found in gravel deposited on the bank of a river. If both lived together Java man is out as a possibility for evolution. The teeth, however, are also said to resemble human teeth in many respects, but to differ in others.

In reporting these "facts" regarding *Homo erectus* and *Australopithecus*, I have tried to be as objective as possible, and to give what seems to be the majority report of current thinking, but authorities disagree one with another, and with their own previous statements not only with regard to opinions about evolution, but also as to brain size, whether tools and fire were actually used by the people or animals which furnished the fossils, or by others who inhabited the cave many years later, etc. About all that we can really say then is that *Homo erectus* and *Australopithecus* once lived and are now extinct. As was discussed in the section on comparative anatomy, one's interpretation will depend on his opinion as to whether similarity proves evolution or one creator with a basic plan. There is also the possibility that it was caused by mutations as we know them today producing degenerate traits in real people.

Neanderthal Man

Neanderthal man has been almost as badly misinterpreted as the Piltdown man. Referring to this, *Encyclopedia Britannica* says, "The popular conception that these people were slouched in posture and walked with a shuffling, bent-knee gait seems to have been due in large part to the misinterpretation of certain features of the limb bones of one of the Neanderthal skeletons discovered early in the 20th century."[41]

This skeleton was that of a Neanderthal man who had in his knees a bone disease which some think was rickets, and others consider arthritis. He probably really did walk with his knees bent. Since this put his posture half way between man and the knuckle-walking apes, his pictures and statues were used to teach evolution for many years, even though many other Neanderthal fossils were found, and all the others walked erect.

41. F. Clark Howell: "Neanderthal Man," *Encyclopedia Britannica*, 1965, Vol. 16, p. 152.

They are now discontinuing the use of Neanderthal man as a link in human evolution. Just as museums had to throw out their statues of Piltdown man, they are now replacing Neanderthal man. The following excerpt taken from an early 1971 issue of the *Portland Oregonian* deals with changing the Neanderthal statues at the Chicago Field Museum of Natural History. It was titled "Status Slowly Rises for Neanderthal Man." (And in an age when you can get to the moon in a couple of days, "slowly" is certainly the term to use!)

> The old idea of neanderthal man was that of a bent-over, knuckle-dragging, hairy, grunting, subhuman who looked for meat through deep-set eyes peering from under a massive bony brow.
>
> For one thing, Cole said, neanderthal man stood as straight as we do. The head was erect, balanced on the spinal column—otherwise, he would have toppled over.
>
> He had a good-sized brain and there was not such a great hump of muscle running from the shoulders up the neck as appears in the old, about-to-be-replaced figure.

Of the biology textbooks checked in 1973, only one still had Neanderthal man's knees bent, though several still suggested that we evolved from him. Most however, favored *Homo erectus* and *Australopithecus* for this honor.

Since a good deal of the argument for evolution of man is based on the smaller brain size of *Pithecanthropus* and *Australopithecus* it is of interest that Neanderthal man had an average brain size about 100 cc. larger than the average of people today which is 1350 cc.[42] It is also interesting to note how unimportant brain size becomes when we are dealing with

---

42. M. F. Ashley Montague, *An Introduction to Physical Anthropology*, 1960, pp. 194-203.

larger instead of smaller ones. Regarding this argument the well-known anthropologist M. F. Ashley Montague writes:

Compared with modern man Neanderthal man is distinguished by a forehead which is much less sloping than it appears to be. The apparent sloping is an illusion created by the presence of markedly developed eyebrow ridges, the supraorbital torus. . . .

In spite of the fact that conclusions relating to mentality drawn from the shape of the normal head have long ago been demonstrated to be utterly valueless, there are still some students who forget themselves so far as to assert that Neanderthal man must have had a poor mind because he had a rather more beetling brow than their own. The fact is that, within a certain range of variation, neither the volume, shape, nor the size of the brain in the Hominidae bears any relation whatsoever to intelligence. Individuals whose brain did not exceed 750 cc. have been recorded who were of perfectly normal intelligence. Persons with low foreheads are known to be not one bit better or worse mentally than those with high ones. . . .[43]

The dates usually given to Neanderthal fossils are from 30,000 to 60,000 B.C. The fossils which are believed to be older are also found to be more similar to modern man.[44] Neanderthal man proves only that man has an awful tendency to force the evidence to conform to his theory. One wonders how many of the other fossil evidences for evolution would bow out if we knew more about them, or if what we know already were not interpreted with an evolutionary presupposition.

---

43. Montague, p. 194.
44. Sir Wilfred Le Gros Clark: "Man, Evolution of," *Encyclopedia Britannica*, 1965, Vol. 14, p. 738.

The Cro-Magnon man made the famous cave paintings purported to have been painted between 30,000 and 10,000 B.C. These paintings show work equal to that done by good modern artists. Especially famous are the paintings at Lascaux in France, which are believed to be from 30,000 B.C. Radiocarbon dating places it around 8000 B.C. instead. Since this does not go well with the theory of the great antiquity of these paintings, these dates are rejected, with the explanation that they just show that the cave was still inhabited.[45] How the paintings could still look bright and pretty after twenty thousand years of being smoked up by the fires of cave men was not explained.

It is interesting that the Cro-Magnon brain size averaged from 1550 to 1750 cc., which is from 200 to 400 cc. larger than those of people today.[46]

The Swanscombe skull found in 1935 is considered one of the older normal human fossils by evolutionists. "Conservative estimates based on geological considerations give an antiquity of not less than 100,000 years, or according to potassium-argon evidence, probably at least 200,000 years."[47] Evidence that there were normal people around before Neanderthal should have shown the evolutionists that they did not evolve from Neanderthal, but it did not seem to do so. The fact that it did not, shows something of the confusion of the human fossil situation. The Steinheim skull is another human fossil believed to be of the same period as the Swanscombe skull.

Hungarian man was found at Vértesszöllös in 1965.

---

45. *Science*, March 1956-August 1957, University of Gronigen Radiocarbon Dates.

46. B. G. Campbell: "Cro-Magnon Man," *Encyclopedia Britannica*, 1965, Vol. 6, p. 792.

47. Clark, "Man, Evolution of," *Encyclopedia Britannica*, 1965, Vol. 14, p. 738.

This fossil is of particular importance since ages of the various strata in this area are considered to be very well established.[48] At the time Hungarian man was dated, he was classified as *Pithecanthropines*, with which the age of 400,000 years assigned to him would agree.[49] Later examination of the fossils has shown them to be *Homo sapiens* instead.[50] Since one of our species was around at almost the same time as *Pithecanthropines*, it makes man's evolution from this source almost impossible, and from the other candidate, *Australopithecus*, very difficult.

In November 1972, Richard Leakey, son of the controversial anthropologist Louis Leakey, announced the discovery of a human skull and thigh bones more than 2.6 million years old.[51] While the discovery was publicized in most newspapers and scientific journals, it is too early at this writing to see how widely it will be accepted. If true, this means that our species was around forty-five times as long ago as Neanderthal man, six times as long ago as *Homo erectus*, and at the same time as *Australopithecus*. This eliminates everything we were supposed to have evolved from!

However, this is not as serious a blow to evolution as it might seem, since many serious evolutionists had already crossed out Neanderthal man, *Homo erectus*, and *Australopithecus* as possibilities, and having run out of anything reasonable to back into, had retrenched to the illusive "common ancestor." Since it seems to be a characteristic of the "common ancestor" that he leaves no fossils, it is harder to prove that we are not his descendants.

Continuing research has shown our species to have already been on the scene at the same time or earlier

48. Coles, J. M., *Archaeology of Early Man*, 1969, pp. 303-305.
49. Oakley, K., *Frameworks for Dating Fossil Man*, 1966, pp. 292-293.
50. Roe, D., *Prehistory*, 1970, p. 46.
51. "The Oldest Man?", *Newsweek*, Nov. 20, 1972, p. 137.

than one after another of its highly publicized "ancestors."

Civilization

History books, radiocarbon dating, and the Bible are all in general agreement as to when civilization began, give or take a thousand years or so depending on what history book, which radiocarbon date, and whose interpretation of the Bible you read. This was around 3500 B.C. in Mesopotamia, and only slightly later in Egypt according to one study using radiocarbon dates.

This makes it difficult to accept the much less secure dates usually attributed to prehistoric man. If man already had a brain larger than ours sixty thousand years ago (Neanderthal's brain was larger than that of modern man), and was so advanced in his ability as to leave drawings that would do justice to a modern painter in an epoch presented as 20,000 to 30,000 B.C., why would he have waited so long to develop the cities and agricultural methods that go with civilization?

The remains of a man's civilization are apt to last longer and be easier to find and date than his bones. While other civilizations such as the Chinese, Aztec, Inca, and Mayan have developed, none was earlier than the Mediterranean civilization. Evolutionary anthropologists for many years felt that the evolutionary process had already developed modern man by 25,000 B.C. at the latest, and some would now push this back to 400,000 B.C., or to 2.6 million years ago. If modern man was really around all this time, we would expect to find that those isolated civilizations which have developed independently of one another would be somewhat spread out over this period. Just one civilization from 20,000 B.C. for example would be a strong proof against the Biblical explanation of creation. The fact that all known civilizations have developed so recently strongly supports recent creation of man.

Population Growth

Another argument that sometimes comes up in favor of evolution is that it allows enough time for the earth to have arrived at its present population, whereas if one believes the Bible account, we would only have those few years from Noah till now, which does not seem like it could possibly be long enough. If we examine the facts, however, we find that known history presents us with a regular tendency toward population increase. The present rate is more than 2 percent a year, with the fastest growth in the more underprivileged areas. This rate is higher than in the past due to better medical care, etc. A rate of only ¼ that, or ½ of 1 percent, would be an average family size of only 2½ surviving children per family, with an average life span of forty years. This is still under the average rate for the one hundred years from 1650 to 1750,[52] which is before there was much benefit from modern medicine, but late enough to have population estimates with some degree of accuracy. If the original pair of people had appeared a million years or so ago, as evolutionists believe, this low rate would allow a present population greater than could be packed into the entire universe. If instead, our present population growth started with Noah's family, it would work out just fine, even using Ussher's date of forty-three hundred years ago for the flood, which is probably the most recent date that anyone would give for it.[53]

Naturally, epidemics, wars, etc., can radically decrease population growth, but it takes a certain popu-

52. Warren S. Thompson, "Population," *Encyclopedia Americana*, Vol. 22, 1950, p. 367.
53. Henry M. Morris, "World Population," *The King's Business*, Jan. 1970, p. 19.

lation level to sustain an epidemic, much as trees need to be close together for a forest fire to spread. It would, therefore, seem that the farther back one goes, the less chance there would be of something of this nature wiping out a substantial percentage of the population, as contact between people becomes less and less.

The argument from population growth, when used against the Biblical creationist viewpoint, is strictly an argument from ignorance. This line of evidence supports a recent creation.

3

Problems of Evolution

We have thus far discussed the evidences for evolution and have found them less than convincing. We want to proceed now to consider the problems of evolution, or what could be called the proofs against it.

The Laws of Thermodynamics

Science has determined some guideposts which have been considered fundamental to an understanding of the world around us and to predicting the direction in which processes can proceed. Among the most fundamental and widely applicable of these are the laws of thermodynamics, the first of which deals with the conservation of energy. The second, which has been just as soundly proved, is that of entropy. It applies here because, among other things, it states the irreversible tendency for processes in a self-contained system to go to a lower order. Otherwise stated, all natural processes lead to an increase in the randomness of the system being considered. Things left to themselves to be operated on by chance, the method by which evolution is said to have come about, do not get more and more organized, but rather more and more disorganized. The entire idea of evolution is contrary to this law of science which in other areas is considered basic to an understanding of the working of things around us.

If evolution actually did occur, there must be some possible biological means by which it could come about. Naturally this has been the object of much thought and experimentation on the part of the evolutionists. Lamarck's thinking on this was that the organism adapted itself to its environment, and that its offspring inherited the characteristics which had been acquired by the parents. Lamarck also felt that organisms developed new organs when they felt the need, and that the extent of their development was proportional to their use. This would be an almost perfect method by which evolution could come about. The idea has been cursed, however, with one insurmountable problem. Things just don't work that way!

With the coming of experimental science, it was soon clear that the changes acquired during the life of an organism are not transmitted to its descendants. If they were, you would have big strong muscles from the hard work your father had done without doing any yourself; your children could play the piano if you had learned how, etc. It does not even work that way for small changes which many generations acquire, notwithstanding the fact that every once in a while some scientist announces he has discovered the contrary in some tiny exception. Science no longer looks to adaptation to the environment followed by transmittal of acquired characteristics as a rational explanation of evolution, though it was quite influential in Darwin's time.

Perhaps the most important aspect of Darwin's theory was the struggle for existence, and the survival of the fittest. The idea here is that organisms which have helpful variations will live to reproduce and pass on their abilities to their descendants. This idea seems good, but it must operate within the limits of the laws of heredity. Since the recognition around 1900 of the value of the work of Gregor Mendel, the father of the science of genetics, scientists have learned much concerning genetic laws, and have found that these do not provide the much-sought method by which evolution could have come about. A look at these will show why.

Mendelian Laws

1. Law of Segregation. In the formation of reproductive cells, pairs of genes controlling a given characteristic separate from each other and go into different reproductive cells.

2. Law of independent assortment. In the formation of reproductive cells, genes for different characteristics (for example, length of stem and color of flower) assort independently of one another. In fertilization they recombine by chance.

Mendel's laws reveal that characteristics which are recessive may skip one or more generations and reappear later. When they reappear they are just the same as they were before, and not a new characteristic which has been added. Except for mutations, what may appear to be something new in an animal or plant is really just a new combination of characteristics which were already present in its ancestry. Contrary to this, Darwin believed there were continuous small variations occurring which were not stable.

Applying Darwin's theory of natural selection to this, organisms with characteristics which make them less able to compete in the struggle for existence, eliminate these characteristics by dying without multiplying. Good characteristics can be passed on by the parents that have them, but they must always be characteristics which were already in existence in the hereditary system. Selective breeding and the struggle for existence can make real changes in successive generations, as has been shown by artificially controlling this process to breed heavy, small-boned chickens, etc.; but that could never be the method of evolution, as it adds nothing new—it merely selects and emphasizes characteristics already present. Life could never have progressed from a simple cell to the complexity which we see now by this method, because nothing new is added.

Polyploidy

Another phenomena which seemed to offer some hope as a possible solution to the means by which evolution might have come about was *polyploidy*. This is the result of an abnormal cell division when a cell receives a multiple of the usual number of chromosomes. It is not hard to experiment with polyploidy because there is a chemical called *colchicine* which will produce it.

Polyploidy usually produces giant plants and it has proved very useful recently for producing fruits and flowers much larger than those which could be produced by normal means. It can also be used to produce what are sometimes classified as new species because they reproduce among themselves but are sterile when crossed with the normal plants which produce them. This method, however, is of little help to evolutionists in their search for the mechanism of evolution, as nothing new is added. It is simply a doubling, tripling, etc. of the same chromosomes which were already there. In addition polyploidy reduces fertility in plants, and is rare in animals.

Mutations

The desperation of the evolutionists' search for a means by which evolution could have come about is shown by the fact that they have been forced to select mutations. They did not select mutations because they offered a good logical possibility, but because those means which had seemed to offer really good possibilities had all been eliminated. One by one, it was shown that these other means could not have operated to produce evolution, because they added nothing new, but just reshuffled those characteristics already present in the mechanism of heredity.

Contained in the nucleus of every cell from the simplest to the most complex, are spiral strands formed like twisted ladders made of deoxyribonucleic acid, which is abbreviated to DNA. These strands are in the chromosomes and contain the genes which chemically control the processes in the cells. Occasionally a small accidental change occurs in the chemical structure of a gene. This is called a mutation. Mutations produce physical and physiological changes in an organism. Most are harmful. Many are lethal. Since most mutations are recessive, their effect does not become evident until an individual has two such genes of the same kind. Animals and plants as well as human beings which have a mutant gene and which survive will pass it on to later generations.

Let's compare DNA with a computer tape carrying instructions which control an automated factory. The genes, which provide a chemical code, could be compared to the individual messages on the tape, controlling the work of the factory. In the factory, the appropriate messages from the tape would be carried to the various machines. In the cell, copies of the appropriate DNA messages are carried by another substance called RNA to the machinery of the cell which produces the thousands of different and highly complex chemicals which are necessary for the life of the cell. In the case of more complex forms of life, this also involves producing chemicals to be used elsewhere in the body.

Copies of the computer tape (or DNA) are made and passed from parent to child as the family reproduces and other "factories" are started.

Now let's imagine that the factories make toy

motor scooters. If an accidental mistake is made as the tape is being copied, the toy motor scooters may come out with a broken handlebar, or without a headlight, but it would be pretty hard to conceive of any accidental mistakes in the message which would make a perfect spare tire and mount it in a handy place. To believe, though, that if enough selected mistakes were made in copying the tape, it would cause the factory to manufacture real motor scooters and then automobiles, and then jet planes would be much like believing that accidental mutations or changes in the genes could evolve a cell into fish, reptiles, birds, and mammals.

It can be put another way:

Supposing typists kept typing out copies of a book on the Mechanics and Construction of an Outboard Motorboat, the atheist wants us to believe that as the typists go on repeatedly recopying, their selected errors would gradually change the book into increasingly high technical instructions for building, say, a nuclear submarine. . . . So, genetically, the crunch for the materialist is this. He believes that instead of these copyist errors developing into a book of complete nonsense as one might have supposed, the language would assume more and more what we would expect from the world's cleverest brains. The instructions for making a sea urchin would increase in size and technology to give precise instructions for making a man.[54]

Actually a living being is such a delicately balanced instrument, with everything having to function almost perfectly for it to remain alive, that the possibility of a really accidental change making it better is much less than the possibility of your dropping your watch on the concrete and making it run better.

54. E. K. Victor Pearce, *Who Was Adam?* 1969, p. 110.

Instead, the harder you throw it down, the less chance there is that it will run at all afterward. The same is true of mutations. The greater the change they make, the less chance there is of the organism's surviving.

What has actually been observed of mutations is that practically all are degenerative, and when they are extensive they are likely to bring about the destruction of the organism.

A very tiny fraction of observed mutations may actually be beneficial. It is possible, though, that most if not all of these are corrections of previous harmful mutations; as, for example, when one drops his watch on one side, bending something in it, dropping it on the other side may occasionally correct it somewhat.

One who has been taught that mutations are the method by which all the wonders of life around us have come into being will probably find it hard to believe what has been said about mutations being harmful instead of helpful. To be convinced of its truth, he need only look at the attitude of scientists toward radiation, which has been proven to increase the frequency of mutations. There was such a fear of the increasing radiation from atomic testing causing more and more mutations, that finally Russia and America, who seldom agree on anything, agreed to stop nuclear testing in the atmosphere. No scientist that I know of wants the tests continued because he thinks the radiation will speed up evolution and make people better, though this would certainly be true if mutations had really brought us up from the single cell.

The harmfulness of mutations seems to be one point on which all scientists are agreed when their own children are involved, even though they may be able to take it on blind faith that at some time in the past mutations made good changes that brought us all the way up from the single cell. This faith, though, contradicts the uniformitarianism on which they must lean for support in the field of geology. If, instead, they say that evolution came about not by accident, but was directed by God, they are fighting not only science but also that which God has revealed to us about how He created. They are following a religion which they themselves have made up.

The Statistical Impossibility of Evolution

If one admits that evolution has been directed by God, it is much more reasonable to accept the explanation which God Himself gives of His creation in His Word, than to say that God chose to create by means of evolution. The majority of evolutionists therefore affirm that all of the progress necessary to bring us along from the single cell to the complexity of life which we see around us came about by completely accidental and undirected changes. There is a branch of mathematics which deals with the statistical probabilities of such undirected accidental changes. It brings to light one of the most interesting and insurmountable problems of evolution.

It is obvious before one really starts his examination that the cards are stacked against the idea that the wonderfully complex living things about us came about by accidental undirected mutations. Mutations are usually small, and the larger ones are often fatal. They are usually recessive. They do not occur very often. They are almost all degenerative instead of evolutionary. Statistically the process of evolution is almost completely impossible.

For it to happen even without these disadvantages would certainly at best require a fantastic length of time. The evolutionists turn this obvious problem into one of their principal weapons. Postulating a period of time so long that no one can understand or imagine it, they say in effect, that in that length of time anything could happen. The average person is hardly in a position to disagree with them.

Though it is true that the length of time the evolutionists propose is long, it is not unlimited. There are ways of calculating the maximum apparent age of the universe—using its rate of expansion for example. Though the evolutionist can imagine great lengths of time, there are some limitations on the length of time that both the universe and the life upon it could have existed. While the number of changes which would have to have taken place to bring life from a single cell to its complexity today is fantastically immense, there are simple enough means of showing whether or not there would have been enough time for them to take place by chance mutations.

Bolton Davidheiser has shown this in a very convincing way. Here is a long quotation from "Of Monkeys, Manuscripts, and Mathematics," to show that the time available to the evolutionary processes was not enough for man to develop by means of accidental changes from a single cell. Whatever method the evolutionist decides to use to determine the age of the world, the time is still too short. Statistically speaking, evolution is an impossible solution to the problem of life as we know it. This is clearly shown in this analysis of one of evolution's illustrations of what accidental changes can and cannot do.

Statements have been made to the effect that if a million monkeys struck at random the keys of a million typewriters for a million years they might write one of Shakespeare's plays. Possibly no one has investigated to ascertain whether there is any validity in such a statement, but as this is easy to do without actually setting up the experiment, let us look into the matter and also let us see if it has any bearing on the problem of evolution.

Suppose we allow a number of assumptions

which will greatly aid the monkeys in their work. We will give them typewriters with only capital letters and some punctuation, so they will not need to capitalize and will not type dollar signs and other unnecessary characters. We will work them in shifts so that the typewriters are going continually twenty-four hours a day and seven days a week, as monkeys do not observe the Lord's day. Although monkeys find the effort of prolonged concentration difficult, we will assume that they type constantly at the rate of five keys per second. We will even assume that they do not lose time while inserting paper into the machines or in changing shifts when one monkey relieves another. Furthermore, let us have a billion monkeys typing at all times instead of a million.

"Genesis," the first book of the Bible, is about twice as long as some of Shakespeare's plays. How much of the Bible could a billion monkeys type in a billion years? Could they write more than Genesis? Could they write as much as Genesis? How long would it take them to write the first chapter of Genesis? How long would it take them to write the first *verse* of Genesis? "IN THE BEGINNING GOD CREATED THE HEAVEN AND THE EARTH." The typing put out by the monkeys in one year would amount to about 158,000, 000,000,000,- 000 letters, punctuation marks, and spaces. If single-spaced on one side of the page, this would be enough typing to make eight stacks of paper from here to the moon. But in one year the monkeys have hardly begun their task.

How long would the monkeys be typing before there was a reasonable chance, say one chance in a hundred, that they had written the first verse of the Bible? The answer is about 120,000,000,000,000,000,000,000,000,000,- 000,000,000,000,000,000,000,000,000,000,- 000 years. So we can say with assurance that a million monkeys typing for a million years would *not* write a play.

A period of time like this is beyond our power to comprehend, but it is not eternity. Suppose one grain of sand were taken from the Sahara Desert each year. The time that would elapse until all the sand had been removed would seem to us a very long time indeed, but it would be insignificant compared to the time the billion monkeys typed in an effort to produce Genesis 1:1.

To illustrate eternity someone once said, "Imagine a rock as large as a mountain. Every day one bird comes and rubs its beak on the rock. When the rock is completely worn away by the birds rubbing their beaks upon it eternity is just begun."

Imagine a rock as large as the whole earth and suppose a bird came once a year to rub its beak on the rock. It would indeed take a long time to wear away so mighty a rock in this manner but it would be a short time as compared with the time during which the monkeys are employed typing. The volume of the sun is about 1,000,000 times as large as that of the earth. Suppose there could be a rock as large as the sun and the earth and the moon and all the other planets and their moons . . . as large as the whole solar system including the asteroids and the rings of Saturn. Suppose once in a billion years a bird rubbed its beak on this rock and suppose it took a billion such visits to wear away enough rock to amount to a grain of the finest sand. When this tremendous rock had been completely worn away the monkeys would still be busy typing. The birds could wear away more than five thousand such rocks before the monkeys had reached a point where there was a one-in-a-hundred chance that they had completed their task. . . .

It is believed by physicists that the first atoms were formed about 3,000,000,000 years ago. Of course it was not until a long time after this that conditions became suitable for life. Most biologists in discussing evolution do not attempt to explain the beginning of life but accept it as a fact and start from there. Professor Lull of Yale said, "Of this momentous event we have no record . . . all we can say of it is that in the fulness of time, when the earth had, in the course of its physical evolution, become adapted to the abode of life, living substances came into being." Modern biologists believe life began on the earth as complex molecules capable of reproducing their kind about 2,000,000,000 years ago. Scientists with all their knowledge and skill have not yet been able to produce such substance.

The simplest known living matter, the viruses, are exceedingly fastidious in their food habits, for they will not grow except in the living cells of higher forms of life. The first simple life, if such it was, had to survive and reproduce and evolve itself into something higher, all without benefit of higher life in which to do it. This seems a difficult thing to accomplish by chance. . . .

Examples of what is deemed to be evolution in our day amount to such things as a change in shades of butterflies' wings, a change in the number and size of projections built by certain microscopic animals on their shelters, and flies becoming immune to DDT. But flies which are immune to DDT are still flies, and amoeba-like animals which put a few more points on their homes can hardly be said thereby to be progressing in the direction of higher forms of life. Some animals and plants can give rise to new types which may be called new species. But this is speciation and not evolution. They do not evolve from a lower group to a higher. Fish do not become frogs in this way.

If someone says seriously that a million monkeys in a million years could produce some literature of merit, we can say that this is foolishness. But when a famous biologist states as a fact that a certain amount of evolution occurred in a specific time we cannot check mathematically to see if this could be so, because the method of evolution has not been satisfactorily explained. For example, J. B. S. Haldane says, "The following stages in human ancestry are quite clear. Four hundred million years ago our ancestors were fish, if you could call them fish, without lower jaws or paired fins." That is, he says it is quite clear that 400,000,000 years ago our ancestors were a type of animal lower than fish. It might seem that even in the same period of time it would be more likely that a billion monkeys would type a sentence of ten words (and some other sentences besides) than that some fish would give rise to men (and a lot of four-footed creatures and birds as well). Without a mathematical basis for making a comparison, and granting that things are not always as they appear, it still seems incredible that there could be so vast a difference in time between that required by the monkeys and that needed by the fish, when the task of the monkeys appears simpler. . . .

The farthest objects that can be photographed by the most powerful telescope are galaxies so far away that the light coming from them takes a billion years to get there, traveling at the rate of 186,000 miles every second. If the monkeys' typing could be placed in the sky at that distance, it would fill the whole sky and there would be very many times that amount left over. The number of letters, punctuation marks, and spaces tapped out by the monkeys would be nearly twice the number of electrons in the universe, as estimated by Eddington. . . .

Does it really matter whether man evolved from the lower forms or whether he was created in the image of God? One author observes that in Genesis man is made from the dust of the ground and that by the theory of evolution his origin was no lower. He concludes, "So long as God is the creative power, what difference does it make whether out of the dust by sudden fiat or out of the dust by gradual process God brought man into being?"

It makes this difference—if man was gradually evolved he is a rising being and is improving. But if man was created and his history is to be found in Genesis, he is a fallen creature in need of a Savior. . . .

The monkeys would have only had to place in their proper order fifty-four strokes of the keys. If man evolved from a single cell, it would have involved putting perhaps millions or billions of changes in their proper order. The monkey illustration clearly shows that the time necessary to achieve an evolution of this order would have been so excessively long as to be a complete impossibility. Notwithstanding the statistical impossibility, it is exactly this accidental type of change which the evolutionists believe has brought into being life as we have it today.

The theory of evolution would probably never have been accepted in the first place had it been known then that acquired characteristics were not inherited, and that evolution would have to depend on accidental mutations for its mechanism. When this was discovered, evolution was already accepted, and to change theories takes time. In addition, to admit the existence of the Creator opens up the area of man's relationship and responsibility to Him, which many may not be ready to move into.

More Serious Statistical Problems

We have just mentioned some of the statistical problems of the evolutionist. Those mentioned are enough to show that faith in evolution is faith, not in a scientific fact, but in a mathematical impossibility. But there are many complications to the statistical problems that to be honest, one should also face before accepting the theory of evolution.

Statistically the problem is greatly multiplied when one considers parasites which are often incapable of living in more than one or a few specific hosts, or the case of plants which are pollinized by only one kind of insect. Here, if the plant evolved through random changes to the point where it was dependent on the insect to reproduce before the insect had obtained either the ability or the desire to do that which was necessary to pollinate it, the plant would have to die out.

When we realize that we are adding this to the fantastic statistical problems already existing, it seems one would be wise to admit that evolution could not be the method by which the world has acquired the great variety of life which we have around us. For those who are not yet convinced, let's consider the next statistical complication, that which arises in cases where both the plant and the insect pollinating it are dependent on the other for life. One illustration is the fig and the wasp that pollinates it. Neither could live without the other. If their present developmental state is the result of millions of years of small random changes, it is hard to imagine their both arriving at the point of being able to maintain the other in life at exactly the same year. This becomes especially obvious as one considers the fantastic complication of the reproductive relationship of these two organisms—much too complicated for description here. Illustrations of this type could be multiplied, but it is sufficient here to merely point out this complication of the problem and move on to more important topics.

We usually think of evolution as an explanation of the origin of life, but when one really examines the theory, the only real response that evolution can give is that it occurred so many years ago that we should not have worried about it. Naturally this is not sufficient for the thinking man whether theistic or atheistic. However, since evolution is the theory of the development of more complex forms of life from simpler forms, after one has arrived in his thinking at the simplest form, evolution can only say that life must have come from nonlife, which is simpler. As with the other problems of evolution, one can accept this as a possibility, as long as he does not ask "How?"

When one asks "How?" his answer is for all practical purposes that of "spontaneous generation," a theory which was very popular before Louis Pasteur. This was the old idea that dead flesh generates worms, stagnant water generates insects, etc. They weren't there before—and now they are, seeming proof that they developed from nothing. However, sterilization was found to stop the process; microscopic forms of life were discovered, etc. From then on the nonexistence of spontaneous generation was considered one of the best proved facts of science.

The evolutionist, however, is forced to contradict this supposedly sure fact of science. His usual explanation is that the first life developed spontaneously in some stagnant pool or in the ocean. Since it does not happen today, he must take it on faith that at some time it did.

How easy this might have been for Darwin, who died in the year of Pasteur's birth, came to me quite forcefully one day, as I was looking into my little boy's microscope, sharing his excitement at being able to see "simple" cells scooting around in a drop of stagnant water. As I looked, I realized that in

Darwin's day, they must have actually seemed as simple as they looked under the toy microscope. Ironically, I had recently read in the newspaper of man's having finally succeeded in synthesizing the simplest enzyme, with only about 100,000 to go to be able to make as many as an ordinary cell produces. These enzymes are used by the cell as catalysts to carry on the chemical reactions needed to produce the many proteins necessary for the life of the cell. The proteins of which cells are made are complicated substances built up from amino acid molecules.

The smallest really living substance known (Mycoplasma hominis H 39) has six hundred proteins made of an average of four hundred amino acid molecules each.

When we are told that scientists have been able to produce amino acids, or even complete proteins in conditions which, given enough time, might have occurred in nature by passing electric sparks through a particular atmosphere, this does not show that life came to be in this way. It is a bit like finding a way that aluminum could have been smelted in nature to show that airplanes came about by natural means. It does not take just a collection of a few proteins to make life. It takes many proteins with complicated interactions among them. Lots of protein can be found in any graveyard or meat market, but protein does not produce life.

At this time, it is estimated that the simplest form of life theoretically possible would need at least 124 different proteins. Even the enzymes needed to produce them are virtually all too complicated for the best scientists in the best laboratories to synthesize at the present time.

Another interesting detail is that the amino acids, which are the basic building blocks, come in two kinds; those with certain atoms attached on the right-hand side, and those that have them on the left. Since the side they attach to seems to be determined by chance, whenever amino acids are produced in the laboratory they are always more or less half right-handed and half left. This is true whether they are produced in conditions in which they might have been produced in nature or not. Though this seems to be a rather inflexible rule, yet no living things have both left and righthanded amino acids! All are left-handed! No one knows why. No one can reproduce it. It is just the way God made them.

If the impossible happened, and the exact proteins needed to produce life came together, it would still not be life. Returning to the airplane illustration, if we imagine that all the parts were formed and then thrown together, it would still not be an airplane. Someone might say, "But if we threw them all into a big sack, and shook then long enough, anything could happen"; but the statement would not be very convincing.

Now we have the foundation laid, and can consider the most serious problems in the evolution of life. If our first airplane did form and function, it would last only a certain length of time, wear out, and eventually decompose. The cell would have the same problem, and there we would be—without life again.

What we would need to form by chance is not just an airplane, but an airplance that has within it a miniature factory that makes airplanes just like it. For the airplane the job is evidently much easier, because even the technology of fifty years ago was able to make airplanes. As far as the cell is concerned, we are just beginning to understand how to make crude imitations of a few of its parts. Even if we took all the money in the world and built the biggest laboratory in the world, and put all of the best scientists in it, they would not yet be capable of doing what evolution is asking of the cell. What had to form by chance is not a "simple" cell, but a cell which contained within it a factory for making "simple" cells.

Even if this happened, the evolutionist's difficulties

would not be over. The cell that was capable of making other cells would eventually wear out and die, and so would the cells it made. It would not only have to make cells for life to continue, but would have to pass along information they needed to make other cells. We can make airplanes because scientists and technicians can write and put into computers the information they need to pass on to others who are or will be working on these projects.

When God made the first cell, He resolved these problems with DNA which we have already discussed. Even the simplest cell is very complicated, and had to be made, organized, and programmed. If this were not true, and life which could reproduce really could form by chance in the right atmosphere, its problems would not be over.

Evolutionists believe that the atmosphere of the earth when life started did not contain oxygen, but that all the oxygen now found in the atmosphere was produced later by plants. This would probably help give a little more time for amino acids and then proteins to come together, as they would not be oxidized. However it would not produce the long periods of time believed necessary by the evolutionists, since most of the materials necessary are quite unstable even when not in the presence of oxygen.

This lack of oxygen provides the evolutionist with another evidently unforseen problem, however. Life on earth could not exist if it were not for a protective layer of ozone in the stratosphere which shields us from the ultraviolet rays which would otherwise be beating down upon us in deadly quantity. This ozone is formed from oxygen in the air.

With today's knowledge of the fantastically complex processes and conditions necessary for cells to live, it seems quite irrational to believe that the first cell, or better, a miniaturized cell factory capable of producing other cells with the same capabilities, arose accidently from nonliving matter.

Every once in a while we hear that scientists have finally been able to develop life in a test tube. Reading a little farther we find that they had not really made life from non-life, but that it was something almost like it, often times one of the substances of which living things are composed. One of the important announcements in this series was that of Dr. Kornberg, who had been able to make a virus. Actually what had happened was that scientists had discovered how a virus is produced, a very complicated and difficult problem which took years of work. Living cells are used by the virus to produce other viruses. Dr. Kornberg had figured out the system to the point of being able to trigger a living cell to produce a virus without using a living virus to do it.

Analysis of science's current knowledge of the virus seems to eliminate it as a candidate for the first life. Though it is simpler than the simplest cell, the virus presents too many problems. It had already been known that its only "food" is living cells. This fact alone is sufficient to disqualify it from being the first life, except for the possibility of this situation having developed during the years. Adding to this problem, the current knowledge that the virus is also dependent on other cells for its reproduction has convinced most scientists that the virus is not the source of life, but a product of life; and at this writing, scientists are not yet agreed as to whether or not the virus should be considered a living thing.

Most of those who believe in evolution would agree now that the single cell rather than the virus must have been the first life from which other forms have evolved. The simple cell may seem at first glance like a fairly simple thing even though it is more complicated than the virus. It is, however, somewhat like looking at a computer. At first glance it is a simple

gray metal box—the sort of thing which one can
imagine could have perhaps just happened by accident all by itself. A more thorough examination,
though, shows the cell, like the computer, to be
fantastically complicated. With all the years of study,
scientists are just beginning to understand a little
about the so-called simple cell. Each year produces its
list of newly discovered complications of which Darwin knew nothing, and which make the idea of its
"just developing out of stagnant water by accident"
even harder to believe.

Dr. Wilder Smith provides this revealing illustration
of the logic involved in disproving God by developing
synthetic life.

> The achievement of synthetic life is being
> awaited with gloating as the final nail in God's
> coffin. But is this reputable logic?

> Every year I publish articles on my syntheti-
> cal experiments in leprosy and tuberculosis and
> report exact methods of synthesis and biological
> testing of the products. Assume now that a
> colleague reads my articles, finds the results in-
> teresting, and decides to repeat the work him-
> self. After a year or so he finds all my methods
> exact (I hope!) and the biological activities of
> the synthetic products correct. He, in turn, re-
> ports his results in the scientific literature and in
> conclusion summarizes that he has repeated my
> experiments, found them correct and thereby
> exploded forever the myth of Wilder Smith's
> existence. I do not really exist at all, for he has
> been able to repeat my work! The logic is, of
> course, pretty well inconceivable! but yet it rep-
> resents the actual position of the Darwinists and
> New-Darwinists today.[55]

---

55. A. E. Wilder Smith, *Man's Origin, Man's Destiny*, 1969,
p. 92.

As a concluding thought for this section, let us say that if science is eventually able to produce life out of that which does not have life, it will not have happened by accident, but as a result of the work of the thousands of top scientists who through the years have studied this problem. It will therefore not prove that life could come about by itself, but instead, that it could be created by an intelligent being. This would not only be the only logical conclusion, but it is also what the Bible has told us all along had happened. "In the beginning God created the heavens and the earth" (Gen. 1:1).

To summarize, evolution's answer to where life came from is to push the first life back a long way in time and to say that the first life was a simple form. The writers of most textbooks seem to hope that the reader will not notice that this explanation has not really given any answer at all as to where original life came from but has only made the problem seem farther away and their inability to answer it seem less obvious and less important.

How the Organs Originated

Darwin said, "If it could be demonstrated that any complex organ existed which could not possibly have been formed by numerous successive, slight modifications, my theory would absolutely break down." [56] Since he knew nothing of mutations, and felt that the variations normally noticed between members of any species were capable of providing the changes needed, evolution did not seem too difficult. However, knowing as we do that these normal variations do not add anything new, but only offer different mixtures of characteristics already in existence, evolutionists to-

---

56. Charles Darwin, *The Origin of the Species*, 1962 Collier Book Edition, p. 182.

day must instead rely on mutations, which are almost always harmful, for the actual changes.

Any organ which we might want to consider is very complicated, and the more complicated an organ is, the more difficult for it to have come about with no intelligent plan. To illustrate the problem, let us take only a tiny part of the ear. We will imagine that whether by plan or happenstance, the outer ear, the eardrum, and the entire inner ear are already in place. All we ask of evolution is that it give us the three little bones that are put together in such a way as to provide a complex lever joining the eardrum and the membrane of the inner ear to make the hearing a little better than it would be without them.

Even if tiny little bones were produced outright by mutations in sufficient numbers that three of them fit together by chance to form a complex lever, they would probably not be in the right place to function and would eventually be discarded. Evolutionists have therefore tried to work out theories by which mutations could modify existing structures so that any organ would be helpful to the organism in every stage of its development so as not to be discarded. In organs with complicated functions this becomes increasingly unlikely. In the case of the ear, it has been postulated that the evolution was from a type of reptile called the therapsid which already had a small bone in its head which carried vibrations from one of the large bones of the head to another. This leaves only two small bones to account for. One of these is supposed to have been provided by the joint of the lower jaw which was on the end of a rather thin bone. It is assumed that this piece of bone came off the jaw, and changed its shape and position to attach to the other small bone which was already there. This left the jaw with the job of developing a new joint. Since one of the bones presumably came from the end of the lower jaw, the other one still to be accounted for is assumed to have come from the upper jaw. How this is supposed to solve the problem of the bones continually adding something to the ability of the animal during the whole process so as not to have been discarded in the struggle for existence is still not clear to me, so I will quote the heart of the best statement on the subject that one of the top research organizations in the United States was able to find for me. Speaking of these last two bones this authority says:

> It takes no great stretch of the imagination to envisage the articular and quadrate (bones) torn, so to speak, between the conflicting demands of the masticatory and the auditory functions—the former calling for massive, stable muscle-clad bones, the latter for delicate air-borne mobile ossicles. If this dilemma of Solomon really existed it follows that the mammals owe their very existence to some unknown therapsid that hit on the inspired compromise of placating the masticatory function with a brand new joint in order to dedicate the bones of contention to the overriding needs of air sensitive hearing.[57]

It seems obvious to me that it was God instead of the therapsid who saw the need and worked out the details. Look where one may, it is difficult to find an organ whose development can really be explained by evolutionary methods.

Reproduction

If we imagine for a moment that something comes into existence by spontaneous generation that is capable of some process of taking in nutriment and changing it into the materials necessary to sustain its

57. Tumarkin, "Evolution of the Auditory Conductive Apparatus in Terrestrial Vertebrates." *Hearing Mechanisms in Vertebrates*, edited by DeReuck and J. Knight. London: J. and A. Churchill, Ciba Foundation Symposium, 1968.

existence, and then to eliminate its wastes, we are then faced with a rather difficult problem. Since reproduction in any form is quite a complex process, it would seem to have required many generations of evolution before the first cell was able to reach this stage of development. What kind of mutations lifted him up to this point? Was it spontaneously generated with genes and chromosomes, often compared to computers because they program and direct the development and reproduction of living things? Because of their complex molecular structure this would hardly seem possible, but if not, how was it able to solve the problem? How did it pass through the number of generations necessary to evolve to the point of being able to reproduce? If it was generated with this ability already built in, we are imagining the spontaneous generation of an already rather complex being. In actual experience, complex functional mechanisms can be destroyed by chance, but are never formed in this way. Evolutionists must at times long for the good old days when the simple cell was really thought to be simple.

If one is able to take it by faith that in some unknown way our first cell was able to surmount this obstacle, then instead of having solved the problem of reproduction, he finds it further complicated. He must now explain the origin of the first organisms that could reproduce sexually. The gap between an organism which reproduces asexually and either a male or a female organism is large enough that it would be hard to think of its having been spanned by only one great mutation. If on the other hand, it took several, we have the same problem as with the evolution of any other organ. That is, "Why did natural selection preserve a characteristic which had no function?" But if one imagines that it did, he gets to the real problem. At the same time that the male was developing by random chance changes, the female must also have been developing independently, and close enough to the same location as to be accessible. In addition, the sex mechanism not only had to be functional in the sense that the female cell once fertilized would go ahead and develop to give life to the first organism produced sexually, but would have to be equipped with a way of bringing the male and female cells in contact. All this though, would be useless and eventually eliminated if at the same time some form of sexual desire was not also evolved. While we cannot accept many of these things that an evolutionist must believe, we cannot help but admire his great faith.

Origin of Matter

Materialists find it hard to believe that God is eternal, yet they feel that matter has always existed. In evolutionary thinking, every stage of development requires an earlier stage. There is good scientific proof, however, that matter has not always existed.

"For example, our sun is losing weight at the rate of six million tons a second. Has this process been going on from all eternity? If so, there must have been a time when the sun was infinitely big, filling the whole of space!"

If stars burn hydrogen or any other material by radioactive means, or any other known means, in an infinite time, it would all be consumed and combustion would cease.

"The sun and all the billions of stars which make up our universe are extremely hot, whereas interstellar space is extremely cold and bodies like the earth are in between. But hot metal (or any other matter) cannot retain its heat in cold water for an indefinite period; it is only a matter of time before the two substances settle down to a uniform even temperature. So if the universe were infinitely old, all matter would long ago have reached an equilibrium of heat. But it is not so; therefore matter cannot be infinitely old or eternal."

Or take the radioactive elements such as uranium for example. These are continually decomposing, and any given quantity will be halved within so many (let us call it "X") years. X years ago, then, there was twice as much uranium in the world as there is now. 2X years ago there was four times as much, and so on, until an infinite number of years ago there was an infinite quantity of any or all of the radioactive elements we would like to choose, which is hardly possible.[58]

The continual expansion of the universe, as the stars and galaxies which seemingly are shooting out as if from some center where they all originated, also implies a time of origin. It is estimated that if the universe expanded at what seems its present rate for even one-fifth the estimated lifetime of the sun, the universe would be virtually empty of visible galaxies.[59] This has been such a problem to the atheist that a few have even accepted a theory that the universe goes through periods of expanding and contracting eternally. The problems, however, in finding some cause for this and the lack of any evidence in its favor have kept it from general acceptance. It does show, though, their recognition that the evidence points to a time of creation, and that the other theories of the universe starting from an explosion or from cooling gasses do nothing to answer the question: "Where did the material that exploded come from, or where did the gas come from?" This theory shows us also the recognition by some atheists, at least, that the usual atheistic response "God did not

---

58. John Wu, *Questions Concerning the Faith*, mimeographed edition, English translation, pp. 11-12.
59. Floyd E. Hamilton, *The Basis of the Christian Faith*, 1964, p. 22.

create the universe" is a little hard to accept, unless one can avoid the overwhelming evidence that it did start sometime. They see the need for a substitute explanation of the beginning, if the normal explanation that God created is to be thrown out. Evolution, as a substitute faith, is rather shallow, and it provides evasion instead of answers to the basic questions.

Order in the Universe

An atheist sat one day on a lovely lawn looking at the blades of grass, the leaves of clover, and the little flowers. The more he gazed on this restful scene the more troubled he became because everywhere he looked, searching for accident and chaos, he found symmetry. Indeed, wherever he might have chosen to look from the tiny atom to the great solar system, instead of chaos he would have found order.

"Consider the earth on which we live. It is tilted at an angle of 23 degrees. If this were not so, the water vapor from the oceans would go to both the north and south poles, condense, and pile up mountains of ice. If the sun gave off half as much heat we would all freeze, while if it gave off twice as much heat we would all be roasted."[60]

"The earth itself is revolving at a speed of 1000 miles per hour at the equator. If it were to revolve at only 100 miles per hour, night and day would increase ten times in duration, plants would be scorched in the day and seedlings would be frozen to death at night.... If the moon were only 50,000 miles away from the earth the tide would flood all lands including high mountains.... If the oceans were deeper, carbon dioxide and oxygen would all be absorbed and no plants could exist. If the atmosphere were thinner than at present, millions of meteors

---

60. Hamilton, *Basis of Christian Faith*, p. 42.

which are burned up in the air would fall to earth and cause terrible fires."[61]

While most things contract when they freeze, water instead expands by about one-eleventh of its volume. This makes ice float on top of a lake, preventing the lake from freezing all the way through and killing all the fish.

The very atheist who argues against an ordered universe unknowingly sets his watch by instruments which in turn have been set by the orderly orbits of the stars tracked by an observatory in England or by atomic clocks, utilizing yet another evidence of the regularity of his environment.[62]

What makes order instead of chaos in the universe? Is it just an accident? One sits in vain in the grass outside the junkyard gate waiting for a watch or a boat or a simple house to form itself from the pile of rusty scrap! No order comes. Order requires that someone set things in order, but the mind which rebels against belief in God must believe that the complex and wonderfully ordered universe in which he finds himself came about all by itself, the result of no mind or plan, like finding a fine Swiss watch formed by an explosion in a junkyard.

The Historic Evidence

Dr. David Willis, professor of biology and chairman of the Department of General Science, Oregon State University, in a paper presented to science teachers involved in the 1972 textbook controversy in California, included this interesting line of evidence:

Let us now consider historical literary evi-

61. Wu, *Questions Concerning the Faith*, pp. 5-6.
62. J. D. Ratcliff: "Where Time Begins," *Reader's Digest*, April 1968, pp. 193-196.

dence. Questions of origin and the past history of life have intrigued men of all times. Most cultures have produced some folklore explaining how life and the earth began. Nearly all such material is fanciful in the extreme and bears no relation to the real world. Multiple deities interacting in bizarre circumstances give rise to the world and its biota in these myths.

Of particular interest are those stories from the Near East, where archeological investigations of literate civilizations have been most extensive. One of the most lengthy and well preserved is the Babylonian creation story recorded in cuneiform on seven clay tablets. Dr. Alexander Heidel of the University of Chicago has produced a complete translation and cogent analysis of these tablets (The Babylonian Genesis). Even a cursory examination of this narrative will show its total incompatibility with a scientific view of the world.

In sharp contrast, the book of Genesis in the Jewish-Christian scriptures presents an abbreviated, but majestic account of the origin of the earth and its organisms. The account outlines in its broader aspects a series of creative actions by a supernatural being (God) that closely parallels present scientific understanding. This cannot be said of any other ancient creation story. Magical and fanciful elements are notably absent. The opening statement sets the tone, "In the beginning God created the heavens and the earth" (Genesis 1:1).

The antiquity of the Genesis account is unquestioned. Its existence raises the obvious question, "How could its author have been so accurate in his statements that thousands of years later it can reasonably be viewed as an acceptable summary of the sequence of events connected with origins?" One cannot pass off Genesis as just a lucky guess, for compared to its contemporary creation stories from surrounding cultures it is unique. This document cannot be dismissed out of hand. It constitutes a valid form of historical evidence. Its very existence and accuracy demand that it also be considered when the problem of origins is examined. . . .

If a supernatural being (God) did oversee the origin of life, and *if* he desired to communicate some summary information about these events to his rational creatures (men), then the Genesis record would seem to qualify. In no other way does it seem possible for human beings to be informed of such events. . . . Furthermore, Genesis claims to be just such a record.

When we realize that even men of genius like Aristotle, living at the highest point of ancient knowledge came up with many scientific blunders, it would seem that an open minded approach should indeed include the consideration of this record.

4

Explanations

*What Can Natural Selection Working on Mutations
Accomplish?*

We have now examined both the "proofs" for
evolution and its weaknesses, and have found evolution inadequate to explain much of the life that we
see around us. Does this mean that natural selection
working on chance mutations can do nothing at all?
The answer is no. There is what seems to be very
good evidence that it can produce real changes over a
period of time. If there were no evidence of change
from these causes, intelligent scientists would never
have accepted the theory of evolution. The evidence,
however, shows only a certain amount of change. It is
always obvious, if one looks for it in honest textbooks, that after a certain point the discussion is full
of such terms as "appear," "would seem," "extrapo-
late," "perhaps," "probably," etc. Evolutionists see
evidence for a certain amount of change such as a
change in the shape of a clam's shell, etc., and believe
that, based on this evidence, they can assume a probable extension on back to a single simple cell. This we
would definitely deny.

In the past many have felt that there had to have
lived a continual sequence of animals intermediate to
those living today, and thus the hunt for missing links
was launched. Little evidence has been found, however, which could be interpreted to provide these

"missing links." Austin H. Clark, himself an evolutionist, put it this way:

> . . . So from all the tangible evidence that we have been able to discover, we are forced to the conclusion that all the major groups of animals at the very first held just about the same relation to each other that they do today. . . . There is strong circumstantial evidence which indicates that none of the major groups could have been derived through any of the others.
>
> A study of the developmental lines of animals shows that developmental progress is always evidenced by increasing specialization along definite structural lines at the expense of other structural features. Organs may gradually become reduced and perhaps disappear, but nothing is ever added. Specialization is always a matter of subtraction from a well-balanced whole. Such subtraction once started may continue, or it may cease, temporarily or permanently. But a structural feature that has once begun to lose importance and to dwindle never reverses the developmental path; it never recovers any of its lost significance.
>
> All of the major groups of animals differ from each other both in the reduction of some of the bodily structures and in the very great development of others. Thus they differ from each other both by subtraction and by addition. To assume that any of the major groups are derived from any of the others is therefore to deny the general application of a well-established principle.[63]

He explains this lack of evidence for one group arising from another by assuming that all lines evolved separately from the first few offspring of the first living cell. Writing on the problem more recently,

---

63. *The New Evolution Zoogenesis*, 1930, pp. 211-213.

G. A. Kerkut attempted to explain the evidence by postulating that instead of only one cell originally starting from spontaneous generation, there have been a number, and that each of these original cells has evolved separately.[64] How much better is God's explanation that He created separate distinct groups which reproduced according to their kind!

Let us look at the Bible's explanation of how God create more than just the simplest form of life. Genesis 1:24-25, for example, declares His creation of the animals: "And God said, Let the earth bring forth the living creature after his kind, cattle, and creeping thing, and beast of the earth after his kind: and it was so. And God made the beast of the earth after his kind, and cattle after their kind, and everything that creepeth upon the earth after his kind: and God saw that it was good." What the word translated here as "kind" would be in our modern classification is not spelled out, but it is clear that in general it fits with the real evidence which science has found from nature. Nature is, after all, another revelation of God and will never really conflict with His revelation in the Bible. Evidence shows some change occurring, but that this is responsible for all of life is only an assumption. Mutations cannot produce changes in an always upward direction, as many evolutionists once believed, but in various directions, and mostly downward. Changing environments give more chance of survival to some of these changes than to others. We do not deny that this accounts for some of the differences in the forms of life about us, but we do strongly object to the vast superstructure of atheistic theory which has been built upon this tiny foundation. It is a superstructure which requires much more faith, and a much less reasonable faith, than God's explanation that He created the first animals, and man.

---

64. *Implications of Evolution*, 1960.

This becomes obvious when one realizes the fantastic disadvantage of a single-celled animal in the world today where every other creature is presumably more evolved and better able to sustain itself in the battle for existence; yet it does not seem to bother our one-celled friends in the least. Billions of them still exist.

What then has natural selection working on mutations actually accomplished? I realize that this is so revolutionary that it seems impossible to many people, but I would suggest that it has accomplished only that which the evidence would seem to show.

The Influence of the Theory of Evolution on Society

Evolution today has an influence far beyond simply being used as an explanation of the origin of the species. It has been imposed upon many areas of life.

In religion it is often stated that man is advancing from a primitive religion of many gods to a belief in only one. In actual practice, however, both beliefs exist together as far back as historical documents other than the Bible can take us, and the Bible explains belief in one God as coming first.

In the field of languages, those linguists who follow the evolutionary theory state that human languages are developing from meaningless sounds to ever more perfect languages. This is evidently necessary if man really did develop from lower animals, but it certainly does not fit the evidence. Modern languages can be traced back to certain families of languages, but beyond this no connection has been found. Those who know modern Greek, Arabic, Hebrew, and neolatinic languages, etc., and also those languages' ancient classical counterparts state that the ancient language was the most perfect. There is need for more research in this area, as the actual evidence seems contrary to the evolutionary theory, but seems to fit well with the Biblical point of view, that God did something which started a number of languages at the tower of Babel (Genesis 11:1-9).

While the theory has had its influence in many areas of life, that which interests us the most here is the area of morality. Evolution provides man with a way to escape his responsibility to God. If everything in existence today has developed without God, then there is no judge before whom we must all appear. In the interpretation of many, man is responsible only to himself, and that which helps evolution helps society.

Hitler used this to rationalize his hatred of the Jews. Sir Arthur Keith, an evolutionist himself, states this point succinctly. "Hitler is an uncompromising evolutionist, and we must seek for an evolutionary explanation if we are to understand his actions." [65] According to Hitler, the Germans were a superior race. If the Jews were left to intermarry with the Germans, the work of nature "to establish an evolutionary higher stage of being may thus be rendered futile."[66] He also expressed his evolutionary ideas in other contexts. For example, "The whole world of nature is a mighty struggle between strength and weakness—an eternal victory of the strong over the weak. There would be nothing but decay if this were not so."[67] ". . . The state has the responsibility of declaring as unfit for reproductive purposes anyone who is obviously ill or genetically unsound . . . and must carry through with this responsibility ruthlessly without respect to understanding or lack of understanding on the part of anyone."[68]

Using evolution as his rationalization Hitler guided one of the most advanced nations the world has ever

---

65. *Evolution and Ethics*, 1947, p. 14.
66. Robert E. D. Clark: *Darwin Before and After*, 1948, p. 115.
67. *Ibid.*, pp. 115-116.
68. Adolph Hitler, *Mein Kampf*, 1933, quoted by A. E. Wilder Smith, *Man's Origin, Man's Destiny*, 1969, p. 188.

known in the massacre of millions of people, of whom many were women and children, and almost all of whom were innocent of any crime against him or his government.

Another evolutionist might well argue that Hitler did not interpret evolution as he should have; that that which happens in a few years, or even a few hundred years has hardly any effect on evolution, but rather it is the long-range effect of thousands of years that really affects evolution. There were undoubtedly many of the Jews in Hitler's day who understood evolution in a long-term way, but they were killed anyway. In addition, Hitler was certainly not alone in his interpretation of evolution, nor has an interest in small short-term effects died out in our day.

The atheistic ideas of theoretical communism differ mainly in their application. Marx said that Darwin's theory has a "support from natural science." [69] To the communists it is not only the Jew, but also the capitalists who are degenerate.

There is often a real difference between the conduct of one who is convinced that God exists and that he is responsible to Him, as he tries to obey God's command to love even his enemies and to treat them as he would like to be treated, and the conduct of one who does not believe in God, but thinks that it would be best for the race to eliminate whomever he happens to consider inferior.

Theistic Evolution

There are those who believe in God, and also in the theory of evolution. They say that God used evolution as His means of creating. They use God as their solution to the problems of evolution. This idea is not acceptable to most evolutionists, since evolution is largely a way of explaining life apart from God; nor is

---

69. Max Eastman, *Marxism: Is It Science?* 1941, p. 92.

it Biblical. Many who have not really studied the subject in the Bible feel that they can believe in evolution and still believe all of the Bible except a small part at the beginning of Genesis. The subject of God's creating, however, is not limited to any one part of the Bible. In just a few minutes I was able to find over sixty passages in other parts of the Bible which speak of this. It is quite clear from these passages that God created not only the world, but also the living things. God created all things (Neh. 9:6; Acts 14:15; Rev. 4:11). Man too was made by God (Job 10:3; Isa. 17:7; Jer. 27:5; Acts 17:24-25). Christ Himself said that God made man (Matt. 19:4; Mark 10:6). The various organs are also said to have been created by God (Prov. 20:12; Ps. 94:9). There are too many passages which list specific things which God created for one who believes the Bible to be able to accept the idea that God only created the first simple cell and then just directed in the development of other forms of life from that cell. Neither has God created the universe and then gone off and left it to go on by itself as others state, but He also sustains it, keeping it from becoming chaos (Col. 1:17; Heb. 1:3). Those who are trying to escape from God are dependent on Him for their very existence.

Some feel that God is some sort of a blind force, who created, and perhaps also sustains the universe, but who does not know them personally. The Bible strips away this idea as well: "He that planted the ear shall he not hear? He that formed the eye, shall he not see?" (Ps. 94:9). This passage goes on to say "The Lord knoweth the thoughts of man," and that He also chastises and corrects, and that blessed is the man who receives His correction.

Men have always sought for ways to escape from the knowledge of God, and the thinking man, who does not want to believe in God as He is, needs some other theory which seems reasonable to him. As long as he can cling to another theory which seems reasonable to him, he feels free to ignore God.

Having seen now that the theory of evolution can really explain very little, it is our hope that the reader will intelligently examine God's revelation of His creation, find it satisfying, and believe in God, not only as his Creator, but also as his Savior.

How Did God Create the World?

While we cannot know exactly how God created the world, there are certain things we should examine which may be helpful. First, it should be noted that the evidence already mentioned overwhelmingly points to the fact that the world had a time of origin rather than being eternal. Since no human being was there to describe this origin, it is reasonable to examine what God has revealed about it in the Bible. Three passages are particularly helpful: "Before the mountains were brought forth, or ever thou hadst formed the earth and the world, even from everlasting to everlasting thou art God" (Ps. 90:2). Here we find it stated that God is everlasting, while the world was created at some point in time. ". . . Things which are seen were not made of things which do appear" (Heb. 11:3). "I have made the earth, the man, and the beast that are upon the ground, by my great power . . . " (Jer. 27:5). While God does not describe in detail the mechanism used to create the world, He does say that it was by His power, and from things which are not visible. What He tells us certainly fits well with what we know of atomic relationships. Matter can be changed into energy as in atomic bombs, but energy can also be changed into matter. It takes a great amount of energy to produce a little bit of matter, but methods are known by which the change can be made. While we cannot state with certainty that this was the means God used to create the world, and that it was to this method He was referring when He said, "I have made the earth, the man, and the beast that are upon the ground by my great power . . . ," at least it is one possible (and simple) explanation, and it fits very well with presently available scientific knowledge. Certainly it leaves less to be explained away, and requires less faith in the unexplained than could be true of any evolutionary theory.

A moral implication would also seem logical here: If God has power to create the world and man, He has power also to judge men when they refuse to accept the righteousness which He has provided for them in Christ. God is righteous, and He has created man to have fellowship with Himself. Since man is sinful, and not righteous, God has provided for man's righteousness in the sacrifice of His sinless Son. He asks man to accept Christ by faith so that at the judgment man might stand before God clothed not in his own insufficient righteousness, but in that sufficient righteousness which Christ provides. (For further study in this area see the books of John, Romans, and Galatians in the Bible.)

The Age of the World

As has been mentioned before, the Bible does not state the age of the world; consequently, several opinions are held by creationists. They can be divided easily into two major groupings: those who believe that the account of the creation of the world refers to six literal days, and those who feel that the six days were a figurative way of referring to indefinite periods of time. Both have some very good reasons for holding the positions they hold.

Arguments for six literal days are:

1. This would seem to be the normal way to interpret the passage (Gen. 1).

104

2. The term "day" when used elsewhere in Scripture usually means literal twenty-four hour days.
3. It is hard to understand the reasoning of the argument of a Sabbath of rest on the seventh day after the six days of work creating the world if they were not six literal days (Gen. 2:2).

This position is not without a problem, for it would appear to demand that the time when God created the world be more recent than geologic and astronomic evidence would seem to allow. Some therefore, who hold this position feel that there was a time gap in the first two verses of the Bible, and the creation account is actually an account of a recreation a long time after the original creation of the earth.

However, most of those who believe that the creation took place in six literal days feel that the creation was quite recent, and that God created things with an appearance of age. They point out that it is not at all in conflict but actually in harmony with God's normal pattern of creation to make things with an appearance of age. They point to the miracles of Christ as an example. In His first miracle recorded in John 2, He changed water to wine at a wedding feast where they had run out of wine. When it was taken to the master of ceremonies who did not know its origin, he commented that it tasted better than the first wine served. Wine, to be good, must be aged, and this wine, made only a matter of minutes before, was better than the other which had been aged. In the same way, when Christ fed the five thousand, He created fish; evidently real fish, which would demand a certain size, proper development of the organs, bones, and so forth, all of which would imply age. There is no indication that anyone could have distinguished between these fish and any other fish, yet one might certainly wonder why He would make them with bones and organs which they never needed.

In the same way, the Bible infers that Adam and Eve were created mature rather than as infants or as lower animals needing to evolve. God has the power to create, and later He created things which had an appearance of age; why not the world, too?

Those who feel that the Bible is not speaking of literal days, but instead, uses the word *days* as a figure for periods of time, or for pictures of parts of creation which God wanted to display, would point out that:

1. Hebrew is more figurative than most languages and we must attempt to understand that passage in the context of the Hebrew in which it is written, rather than in that of our own language.

2. The Bible says ". . . one day is with the Lord as a thousand years and a thousand years as one day," indicating that God is not particularly limited to time as we see it. This is mentioned in a context which also speaks of the creation of the world, even though more particularly the reference is to the flood in the time of Noah, which it uses as a warning for those who now feel that God will never judge them, just because He has not done it yet (II Peter 3:8).

3. The main reason though that most would feel that Genesis does not refer to literal twenty-four hour days is that they believe that it fits better with the evidence from outside of the Bible of a great age for the earth.

The Worldwide Flood at the Time of Noah

Many things which are otherwise impossible to account for satisfactorily can be explained if one accepts a worldwide flood. The existence of the flood is denied by evolutionists, not so much for lack of evidence, as because of the necessity of keeping to strict uniformitarianism in order to provide more time for evolution. Almost all who believe the Bible believe that there was a worldwide flood and find it to fit well with the physical evidence. Those who believe in a literal six-day creation often feel in addition that the flood accomplished in a short time many things which otherwise would have taken much longer.

We have previously mentioned the difficulty of forming many of the fossils by really strict uniformitarian means, yet there are many examples of great deposits of fossils in existence: the Sicilian hippopotamus beds, the fossils of which are so extensive that they have actually been mined as a source of commercial charcoal; the great mammal beds of the Rockies; the dinosaur beds of the Black Hills and the Rockies, as well as of the Gobi Desert; the astounding fish beds of the Scottish Devonian strata; and on and on.[70] A flood would certainly seem to be the easiest way by which a great number of animals could be concentrated in the same deposit. As the water gradually rose, they would move toward higher ground, where they would be grouped together on the mountain tops, to be swept off together, and deposited by the currents along with loads of sediment.

Describing deposits in central Germany, Newell says: "More than six thousand remains of vertebrate animals and a great number of insects, mollusks, and plants were found in these deposits. The compressed remains of soft tissues of many of these animals showed details of cellular structure, and some of the specimens had undergone but little chemical modification. . . ."[71] He then goes on to tell about feathers, hair, scales, and even stomach contents being clearly preserved. Surely it would take the immediate covering of a great flood to preserve these details, and

---

70. Whitcomb and Morris, *Genesis Flood*, p. 161.
71. N. O. Newell, "Adequacy of the Fossil Record," *Journal of Paleontology*, Vol. 33, May 1959, p. 49, cited by Morris in *Genesis Flood*, p. 160.

explain their compression. By normal processes they would have been completely decomposed. A flood is also necessary to explain the mixture of water and land animals found there and in many other locations. It is possible that the flood at the time of Noah explains many things which are very difficult to explain apart from it.

It would be natural in a flood for the smaller fossils to be deposited on lower levels, and the larger in higher strata, as the water sifted the materials. This action of the water is visible on most beaches where one finds big rocks and logs on higher ground, while moving on down there are smaller rocks and then sand. This action is not perfect, though, and there is usually some mixing of the materials, and occasionally a great deal.

A problem for uniformitarianism which is naturally explained by the flood are the trees which are found here and there fossilized while still standing upright and penetrating several strata. Some, having turned to coal, actually extend through two or more seams of coal and have sedimentary material between them which it would seem by uniformitarian processes would have required great lengths of time to form. [72] The flood would furnish the natural explanation for the rapid deposition of material necessary to cover the trees before they decomposed and toppled over.

The fossils of clams and other marine life found in land areas far from the ocean are also of interest. Since, if there were no marine fossils on land areas, it would be proof against a universal flood, their presence supports the flood, even though it can also be explained in other ways.

In addition to the geological evidence for the flood, there are also other types of proofs. Stories of the flood are found among the oldest documents of many widely separated peoples of the earth. While

---

72. Whitcomb and Morris, *Genesis Flood*, p. 165.

these stories were often handed down for many generations before being written, and contain some details which conflict with the Biblical account, their general agreement on a flood which covered the world and through which one family was preserved is amazing. Since every living people is descended from that family, the normal explanation for the widespread existence of the story is certainly that it was handed down from generation to generation among the various descendents. Especially famous among these is the Babylonian flood story.

Robert L. Whitelaw, Professor of Nuclear Engineering, Virginia Polytechnic, has analyzed the fifteen thousand dates determined by the radiocarbon method and found an abrupt drop in the number of specimens of men, of animals which would be affected by a flood, and of trees during the period dated by radiocarbon to around 3500 to 4000 B.C. (which he feels would actually have been slightly more recent). The drop was to around 13 percent of the number of dates found for the corresponding preceeding period. The number of dates then gradually increases until, by the time of Christ, the number of dates for men and animals is back to where it was before the flood. In the case of trees, the sudden drop and then gradual increase is the same, except that it never gets as high again as it was before the drop.

This clearly points to some great tragedy at approximately the time that the Bible and other accounts speak of the flood. The logical conclusion seems to be that this drop in C14 death dates was caused by the flood wiping out the major part of the nonaquatic living things, and thus not leaving succeeding generations to be dated until they gradually multiplied after the flood.[73]

---

73. Whitelaw, "Time, Life and History," *Creation Research Society Quarterly*, pp. 59-71.

According to the Bible, it did not rain before the flood. Instead, the land received water in the form of a mist (Gen. 2:5-6). While only this statement is made and no extended description of this condition is found in the Bible, yet it seems to suggest the existence of a considerably different set of atmospheric conditions than we have today. The atmosphere evidently held more water vapor than it does today. This would certainly have had its worldwide effect on the climate, tending to produce a greenhouse effect, passing the sun's rays but not allowing as much of the reflected heat to escape. This situation would certainly present a rational explanation for the well-known evidence which many scientists feel points to a time in the world's history when there was a universally warmer climate. The sudden breakup of this atmospheric condition at the time of the flood would not only have provided some of the water, but this, combined with the mixing of a worldwide flood, would further explain fossils of tropical plants and animals found in arctic regions. The rapid freezing of mammoths and other animals found in Siberian fossil beds could only be explained by some such sudden climatic change.

Critics have tried in every way possible to discredit the flood. Since their criticisms have found such wide acceptance, we must respond to the most important of them.

1. Many have been convinced that there is not enough water in the world to make the flood possible. Since we live only on the earth's land masses, it is sometimes hard to realize that most of the earth's surface is covered with water. Over 71 percent is water and its average depth is over 12,500 feet.[74] It is obvious that there is plenty of water. The problem is that people have a tendency to interpret things to fit with what they want to believe. The Bible says,

---

74. *Collier's Encyclopedia*, Vol. 18, 1964, p. 59.

"all the fountains of the great deep were broken up . . . " (Gen. 7:11). One who does not want to believe the flood was possible needs only to feel that this does not mean that anything happened at all, and that all the water for the flood was that which came down in rain. While the atmospheric conditions before the flood would no doubt have provided more water to add to the flood than would atmospheric conditions today, it would still be insufficient to cover the earth as it is now. However, if the fountains of the deep breaking up means that the bottoms of the seas were raised, there would have been plenty of water. Another factor which must be considered is the well-known fact that most of the earth's mountains are of recent formation. At the time of the flood the mountains were very possibly not as high as today.

2. Some maintain that the flood to which the Bible refers was only a local flood, not universal. The Bible, however, says that " . . . the waters prevailed exceedingly upon the earth, and all the high hills, that were under the whole heaven were covered" (Gen. 7:19). Even if the high hills were then a great deal lower than they are now, even if they were only a few hundred feet high, it would be impossible to keep them covered with a flood which lasted a year, without the force of gravity causing the water to find its own level and cover the whole world. You just can't stack water in one spot! Saving the family of Noah and the animals in the ark would not have been necessary either had the people and animals in other parts of the world not been drowned in the flood. The very length of time that the flood covered the earth also argues that it was universal, as it would be very difficult for a flood to last a year in one restricted locality.

The flood is also mentioned in the New Testament. There Peter uses it to illustrate the fact that in the future God will destroy the world with fire. This passage, which points out the folly of those who deny the intervention of God and try to account for everything on a purely uniformitarian basis, loses its meaning if there were not a worldwide flood which destroyed the unrighteous.

> Knowing this first that there shall come in the last days scoffers, walking after their own lusts, and saying, Where is the promise of his coming? for since the fathers fell asleep, all things continue as they were from the beginning of the creation. For this they willingly are ignorant of, that by the word of God the heavens were of old, and the earth standing out of the water and in the water: Whereby the world that then was, being overflowed with water, perished: But the heavens and the earth which are now, by the same word are kept in store, reserved unto fire against the day of judgment and perdition of ungodly men (II Peter 3:3-7).

3. The ability of the ark to carry all of the animals assigned to it has also been called in question. As with most of the arguments considered, men tend to protect their presuppositions by the conditions which they propose. One, for example, spoke of the difficulty of providing water in the ark for all the amphibians. I mention this simply to show that you can't just multiply the number of the million or so different species of animals in existence today by two (male and female) to find the number of animals in the ark. About eighty-eight thousand species are shell fish of one type or another. Many others are worms, fish, etc. which normally live in the water, or are so small as to be saved on floating bits of debris.

Ernst Mayr, a leading taxonomist, lists only 17,600 species of mammals, birds, reptiles and amphibians combined. Many of these could live quite well out of the ark. Of mammals he lists only 3,500 species, and some of these are aquatic.[75]

The smaller animals do not give much of a space problem, and the large ones are not too numerous. Then too, whether one believes that God had the largest or smallest animals of each species come into the ark depends on whether or not he wants to believe there was room for them. Even if God were no more intelligent than man, He would have known enough to send the smaller animals of each species, and of these the young ones, not just to take up less space, but also for maximum reproduction to replenish the earth after the flood. Imagine that Noah had had to carry the 17,600 species mentioned. Since more than half of them are birds, it is obvious that the average size would be very small.

An average two-tiered stock car used to transport sheep, will hold 240. Thus 146 cars of this size would be enough to hold two each of the whole 17,600 species if they averaged as big as sheep, which they almost certainly would not. The ark was 300 cubits long and 50 wide. While the length of the cubit varied somewhat in various times and nations, using the shortest cubit, the ark was 437.5 feet long, 72.9 feet wide, and 43.75 feet high, or a total of 1,396,000 cubic feet, the equivalent of 522 stock cars. This leaves 376 cars for food and people. (No extra was allowed for the "clean" animals of which seven pair went in instead of one because the aquatic and amphibious animals would certainly more than offset this.)[76]

---

75. Whitcomb and Morris, *Genesis Flood*, p. 69.
76. Whitcomb and Morris, *Genesis Flood*, p. 10.

Conclusion

We have examined the reasons for not believing in
God as creator, and have found them to be unsatisfac-
tory. We found instead the reasons for believing in
God as creator to be factual and convincing. The facts
support the Bible! The Bible does not stop with the
creation. It begins with it, and goes on to give meaning and practical guidance to your life.

God has created you in His image to have fellowship with Him. Your sin has broken this fellowship.
You are not in a process of evolution which will
enable you to create your own paradise here on earth.
Instead, technical progress has provided men with
new ways of sinning against one another and against
God. You too have fallen into sin. It was for this that
Christ died in your place on the cross. He paid for
your sins. The flood which destroyed the sinners in
the time of Noah is your warning of the judgment
which will come upon you too if you do not accept
the salvation which God offers you. One family was
saved from the flood because its members put their
faith in the salvation which God offered them in the
ark. Christ is the ark which God offers you. Put your
faith in Him and you will be saved. You will enjoy
the fellowship with God for which you were created.